PUBLIC LIBRARY

# CENTURY

OF

# SCANDAL

© Haynes Publishing, 2010

The right of Geraint Humphreys and Sally Humphreys to be identified as the authors of this Work has been asserted by them in accordance with the Copyright, Designs & Patents Act 1988.

All rights reserved. No part of this publication may be reproduced, stored in a retrieval system or transmitted, in any form or by any means, electronic, mechanical, photocopying, recording or otherwise, without prior permission in writing from the publisher.

First published in 2010. A catalogue record for this book is available from the British Library

ISBN: 978-1-844259-50-2

Published by Haynes Publishing, Sparkford, Yeovil, Somerset BA22 7JJ, UK
Tel: 01963 442030 Fax: 01963 440001 Int. tel: +44 1963 442030 Int. fax: +44 1963 440001
E-mail: sales@haynes.co.uk Website: www.haynes.co.uk

Haynes North America Inc., 861 Lawrence Drive, Newbury Park, California 91320, USA

All images © Mirrorpix

Series Editor: Richard Havers
Copy-editor: Elizabeth Stone
Proofreader: Rebecca Ellis
Creative Director: Kevin Gardner

Printed and bound by J F Print Ltd., Sparkford, Somerset

# CENTURY

## OF

# SCANDAL

A COLLECTION OF OUTRAGEOUS, SHOCKING AND
UNFORGETTABLE INDISCRETIONS...

WRITTEN BY GERAINT HUMPHREYS AND SALLY HUMPHREYS

EXPOSED!

THE GREAT
COVER-UP

PRISON
SCANDAL

CORRUPTION

**LIAR !**

**JAIL BOOZE AND SEX SCANDAL**

# CONTENTS

THE DAILY MIRROR

MAN BITES WIFE!

# INTRODUCTION

Scandals are found in every walk of life, and can affect anybody. They are not the sole preserve of politicians, sports stars and celebrities.

Most of us have a skeleton or two hiding in the closet, and that is exactly where we want them to stay – because once a secret is exposed, everybody has an opinion.

The notoriety provided by a scandal is not always a bad thing, of course. Scandals can make as well as break careers, regardless of whether the allegations are true. They can also increase ratings, sell newspapers and help products fly off the shelves.

On the other hand, some scandals are *so* disgraceful that the moral sensibility of society is said to have been offended. In these cases, the whistle-blown scandal is probably a good thing – sometimes the truth needs to come out in order to avert disaster (or halt it before it spirals further out of control…).

One thing that cannot be denied is our ability to consume scandals. A quick glance through the ages indicates that scandals have been circulating since the invention of the printing press, and almost certainly before. Meanwhile, the rapid proliferation of tabloid magazines, television channels and gossip blogs simply suggests we are far from tiring of them.

To mark this fact, *Century of Scandal* is here to take you on a guided tour through some of the best-known scandals of the past 100 years – please enjoy, but remember: next time, the star of the scandal could be you.

# DRUGS AND ALCOHOL

"IT IS EASY TO GET A THOUSAND PRESCRIPTIONS BUT HARD TO GET ONE SINGLE REMEDY."

**CHINESE PROVERB**

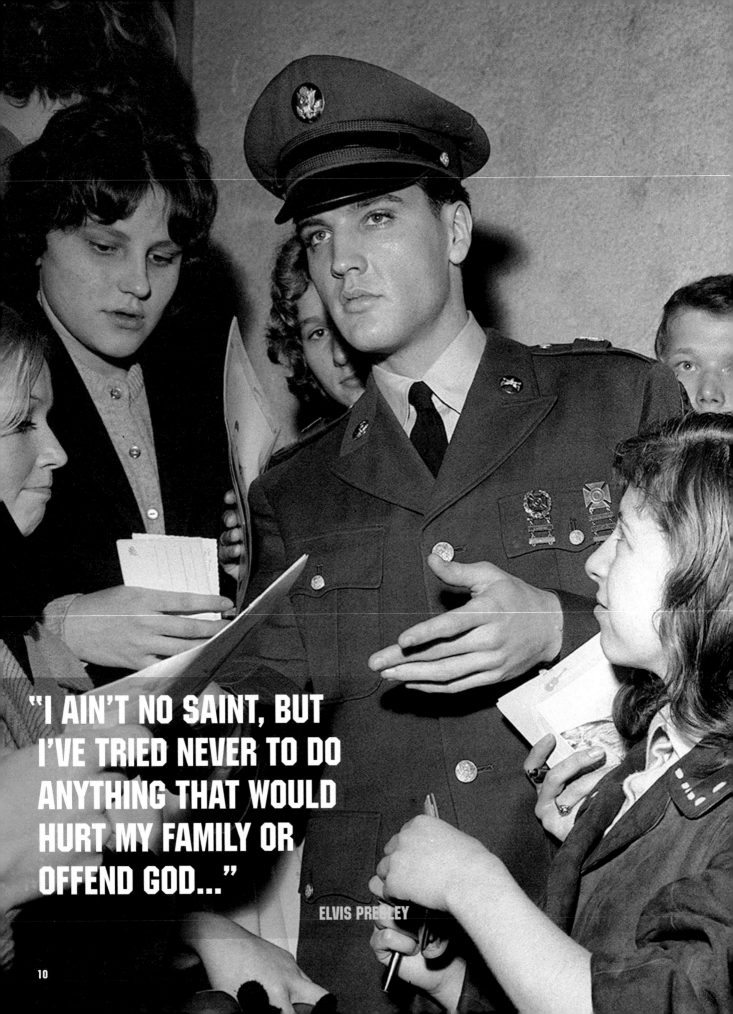

"I AIN'T NO SAINT, BUT
I'VE TRIED NEVER TO DO
ANYTHING THAT WOULD
HURT MY FAMILY OR
OFFEND GOD..."

ELVIS PRESLEY

# ELVIS PRESLEY

Elvis Presley's first encounter with scandal came in 1956 – his performance on *The Ed Sullivan Show* was deemed too sexual for a young audience, and legend has it that the show's cameramen were ordered to film him from the waist up in order to spare the viewers' blushes.

Elvis' distinctive musical style was also controversial, as conservative types found his blend of so-called "black" and "white" genres highly inappropriate. Naturally, complaints like these simply propelled him to superstardom, and Elvis went on to become one of the best-selling artists of all time. Simply put, he was The King of Rock 'n' Roll.

Unfortunately, Elvis' army of followers had to watch as their idol descended into a haze of booze, food and prescription drugs. By the late 1970s he was labelled a caricature of himself as he struggled to finish concerts, and it was apparent that his health was deteriorating inexorably. Eventually, his body simply gave up – Presley passed away on August 16th 1977, aged 42.

# He ate nothing but a.. HOT DOG

CENTURY OF SCANDAL DRUGS AND ALCOHOL

**BELOW:**
A memorial service was held for Elvis in London, August 1977. Thousands of fans gathered outside the church in Cockfosters to pay their respects.

GRACELAND MANSION TOURS

BEGIN JUNE 7th.
For Reservations...
Call 1 332-3322 or (800) 238-2000

It was widely accepted for many years that Elvis' death was the result of an overdose, but a 1994 investigation established that a heart attack was the real cause. It also stated that prolonged drug abuse was a major factor in the onset of his heart problems. Presley's personal "Dr Feelgood", Dr George Constantine Nichopoulos, was eventually barred from practising medicine in 1995, though he insisted he only over-prescribed to The King because he "cared too much".

## Elvis Aron Presley

BORN: Tupelo, Mississippi, January 8, 1935
DIED: Memphis, Tennessee, August 16, 1977

# In peace at last..

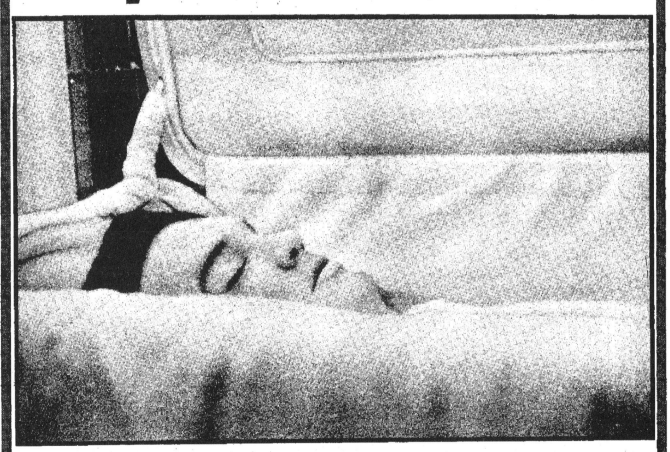

# .. the troubled King

THIS was the world's last glimpse of Elvis Aron Presley. At rest after the turbulent years in which he rose from the poverty of a two-room Mississippi shack to become the King of Rock Music. The picture was taken two days after his death as he lay in a steel-lined copper coffin in the music room of Graceland, his sprawling Memphis mansion, while thousands of fans filed past to pay their tributes—and to see him, like this, for the last time. His later years had tragically been filled with fantasies, furies, private fears. But this is how they, and millions more throughout the world, will prefer to remember him: The King at peace. At last.

13

# Movie star River dies after coke party

## FIGHT BY PARAMEDICS FAILS TO SAVE IDOL, 23

CENTURY OF SCANDAL DRUGS AND ALCOHOL

**From JOHN JAMES in New York**

BRILLIANT actor River Phoenix dropped dead on a Hollywood pavement yesterday – minutes after snorting cocaine at a wild Halloween party.

Sobbing friends told paramedics who battled to revive him that the 23-year-old screen idol was taking the drug as they bopped the night away at the Viper Room – his buddy Johnny Depp's nightclub. Captain Ray Ribar, who spent 15 minutes pumping Phoenix's heart, said: "This case is a prime example of what cocaine can do to some people. It just nails them and stops the heart."

*River collapsed as he left the Sunset Boulevard club at 1am with two girls and a group of men thought to include his younger brother Leaf.*

### Grief

He was declared dead 51 minutes later at the Cedars Sinai hospital after resuscitation attempts failed.

River' parents John and Arlyn Phoenix – members of a cult who named their children in the flower power era – were told of the tragedy at home in Florida.

River had been known as ultra-clean-living. He was a strict teetotaller and vegan who used nothing that originated from animals – including eggs, cheese and honey.

*The 5ft 10ins blond first hit the headlines as a boy in the "coming of age" movie Stand By Me.*

### Best

He was given rave reviews for The Mosquito Coast, co-starring Harrison Ford.

And My Own Private Idaho, which saw him and Keanu Reeves play rent boys, won him the 1991 Venice Film Festival's best actor award.

*This week he was due to start work on Interview With The Vampire alongside Tom Cruise and Britain's Anouk Fontaine.*

**Rave special – Page 11**

RAVE REVIEWS: River with Harrison Ford in The Mosquito Coast

RATED ROLE: Award-winning Phoenix in My Own Private Idaho

14

# RIVER PHOENIX

Hollywood was rocked by the death of rising young movie star River Phoenix.

His credibility as an actor had been established with mainstream hits such as *Stand By Me* and *Indiana Jones and the Last Crusade*, while his liberal views and musical side-projects made him a hit with disaffected teens. The accidental heartthrob was also a staunch vegan who espoused the virtues of clean living, yet on 31st October 1993 he died of a drug overdose while partying at the Viper Room, an LA nightclub partly owned by fellow actor Johnny Depp.

Phoenix had gone into the club's bathroom with friends and taken a lethal cocktail of heroin and cocaine known as a speedball. He instantly complained of feeling unwell, but managed to make his way outside where he collapsed in front of brother Joaquin and girlfriend Samantha Mathis. They tried in vain to hold his body down as it thrashed violently on the pavement, but his heart stopped beating before paramedics arrived. All efforts to resuscitate him proved futile, and Phoenix was pronounced dead at the scene of his collapse.

Many speculated that Phoenix's unorthodox childhood was to blame for his descent into drug use. He and his four younger siblings were for a short time brought up by the Children of God, a cult known for its sexual abuse of minors. He told *Details* magazine that he lost his virginity aged just four, adding, "I've completely blocked it out. I was celibate from ten [by which point the family had left the cult] to fourteen."

Another scandal erupted when unauthorized photographs of Phoenix's corpse were sold to an American tabloid. The Phoenix family did their best to avoid sensationalizing the matter any further by refusing to discuss River's passing, though a number of American rock bands – including REM and Red Hot Chili Peppers – penned tributes to their friend.

"I KNEW THAT MY WORLD
WAS OVER... THAT WAS IT.
THE REST OF MY LIFE."

COURTNEY LOVE

# KURT COBAIN AND COURTNEY LOVE

Courtney Love discovered she was expecting Kurt Cobain's baby in January 1992. That month also saw his band Nirvana ousting Michael Jackson's *Dangerous* from the top of the billboard chart with their breakthrough second album *Nevermind*. Nirvana's record was selling 300,000 copies a month, while Love's band Hole was on the verge of signing a million-dollar record deal themselves. Naturally, Kurt 'n' Courtney quickly became alternative rock's pin-up couple – but they were rapidly heading for scandal.

Cobain was a heavy user of intravenous drugs who frequently overdosed, detoxed and relapsed. Despite his joy at impending fatherhood, he was finding it impossible to stay clean; he suffered from a crippling stomach condition that baffled doctors and led him to self-medicate with opiates and pills. Meanwhile, Love – who had successfully stayed sober since learning of her condition – was desperately trying to keep him on the straight and narrow. Against this chaotic backdrop, the couple married in late February 1992.

Love enjoyed a healthy pregnancy but struggled with the stress and temptation that resulted from having an addict husband. However, in yet another determined bid to get clean for his unborn child, Cobain agreed to a medically assisted detox one month before Love's due-date. The process was almost too much for his body to bear, and so it came to pass that Love and Cobain ended up in different wings of the same hospital when she went into labour that August. Love later stated that she ended up comforting Cobain through his withdrawal while she gave birth.

Unbelievably, this wasn't the most scandalous aspect of their daughter Frances Bean's delivery. Shortly before her arrival, *Vanity Fair* published a torrid exposé on Love, falsely intimating that she had continued to use heroin despite knowing she was pregnant. Love was devastated; she had given several interviews to *Vanity Fair*'s Lynn Hirschberg, with whom she thought she had a genuine rapport. These feelings dissipated immediately when she read the article, because Love knew it was simply a matter of time before social services came calling to check on Frances' welfare. She later admitted: "The power of [the article] was so intense. It was unbelievable. I read a fax of it and my bones shook. I knew that my world was over. I was dead. That was it. The rest of my life. Not only was I going to walk around with a big black mark, but any happiness that I had known, I was going to have to fight for, for the rest of my life. It shouldn't be that way, but I exposed myself to it. Had I not taken drugs in the first place, I would have been lucid enough to know what [Hirschberg] was about. I wouldn't have been candid. I would have figured out where I fit in the scheme of the *Vanity Fair* world."

As expected, the story prompted social services to pay Love a visit while she recovered in hospital with Frances. At just two weeks old, the baby was placed in the care of Cobain's family while Love and Cobain were investigated. They were allowed to take her back when the

# Kurt's baby is only thing keeping me on this planet

investigation was dropped two months later.

Sadly, Cobain's drug use escalated, and in mid-1993 he began to amass a private arsenal of guns. Love had him arrested on trumped-up charges of domestic assault in the vain hope that police would confiscate the guns, but her plan failed. She then staged an intervention with Cobain's bandmates and he eventually agreed to enter rehab the following year – but this would be his final attempt. He climbed the wall of the facility he was staying in and fled to his home in Seattle, taking one last hit

18

of heroin before ending his life with a self-inflicted gunshot wound to the head. He died on 5th April 1994, aged 27.

Against her wishes, Love had been advised to stay away from her husband while he was in rehab, meaning he was alone when he escaped. Tragically, it also ensured that his body went undiscovered for two days. It was only when an electrician called to carry out maintenance work that the grim discovery was made.

There was a global outpouring of grief from millions of Nirvana fans when news of Cobain's death was released, and some blamed Love for his demise. She appeared to make matters worse by refusing to play the grieving widow, throwing herself into work and achieving great success with Hole. She was also critically acclaimed for her turn as Althea in the film *The People vs. Larry Flynt*.

Although Love had shown strength in the face of adversity, she relapsed and suffered a protracted public breakdown between 2000 and 2004, at which point a sympathetic judge spared her jail by ordering her into rehab. Love was typically frank about such troubles when it came to promoting her memoirs in 2006, introducing the book by writing: "You will notice the absence of anything much for about four years of my life; that's because I was on drugs and nothing I wrote made any sense … I never grieved properly for the death of my husband and it finally caught up with me in 2000."

Courtney continues to make the headlines – in 2008 she outraged Nirvana fans by throwing a suicide-themed party for Frances' 16th birthday; a few months later she claimed that ID thieves had completely looted Cobain's estate by buying several properties in his name. She explained: "[the fraud has] been going on since when I went cuckoo, bananas, in 2003."

**ABOVE:** Cobain's body lies spreadeagled on the kitchen floor. A crouching detective takes notes amid the debris.

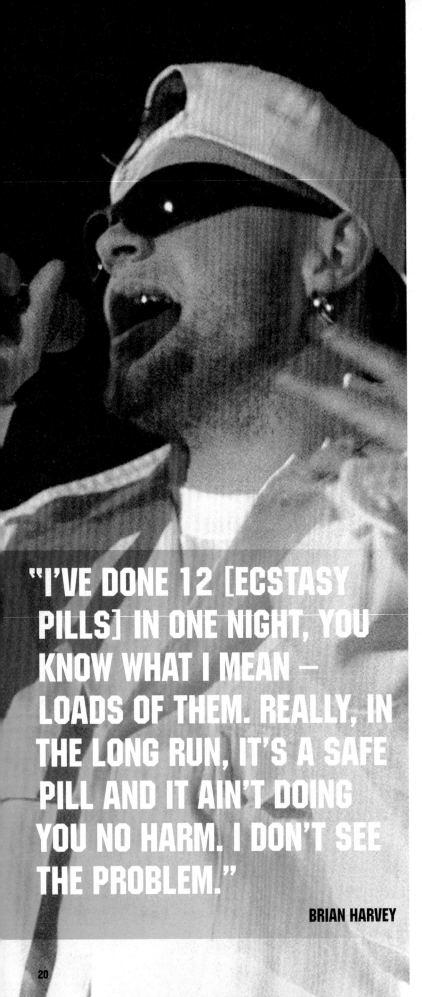

"I'VE DONE 12 [ECSTASY PILLS] IN ONE NIGHT, YOU KNOW WHAT I MEAN – LOADS OF THEM. REALLY, IN THE LONG RUN, IT'S A SAFE PILL AND IT AIN'T DOING YOU NO HARM. I DON'T SEE THE PROBLEM."

**BRIAN HARVEY**

# BRIAN HARVEY AND NOEL GALLAGHER TALK DRUGS

1990s boyband East 17 were always more edgy than their squeaky-clean peers – but nobody was prepared for the media storm that greeted frontman Brian Harvey in 1997 when he appeared to claim that ecstasy was "safe".

The drug was very much in the headlines at the time due to the ecstasy-related death of British teenager Leah Betts, and one year after this tragic event Harvey unwisely announced: "I've done 12 [ecstasy pills] in one night, you know what I mean – loads of them. Really, in the long run, it's a safe pill and it ain't doing you no harm. I don't see the problem."

Harvey's bandmates clearly *did* see the problem, and the singer was immediately fired. The band regrouped under the name E-17, but struggled without Harvey and split soon afterwards. Despite the furore, Harvey found an unlikely ally in the shape of former Oasis guitarist Noel Gallagher, who was disgusted by the public reaction to his comments. He reasoned, "If Brian Harvey did do 12 Es in one night – if he did do, and he's saying that he did – if he's being honest, then fair enough.

"If you can't be honest in this country then we might as well go and live in China, know

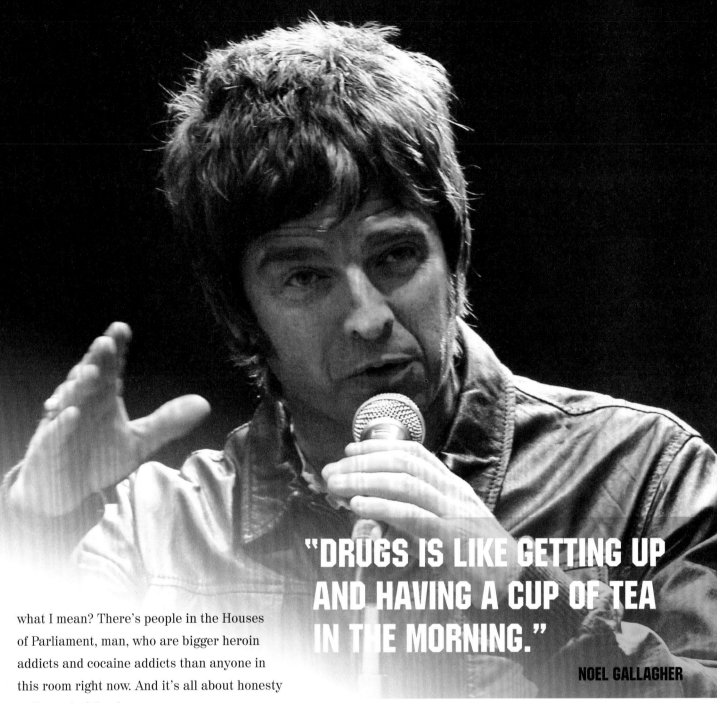

**"DRUGS IS LIKE GETTING UP AND HAVING A CUP OF TEA IN THE MORNING."**

NOEL GALLAGHER

what I mean? There's people in the Houses of Parliament, man, who are bigger heroin addicts and cocaine addicts than anyone in this room right now. And it's all about honesty at the end of the day.

"As soon as people realize that the majority of people in this country take drugs, then the better off we'll all be. It's not like a scandalous sensation, or anything like that. Not when you've got our Government selling arms to people who go out and kill probably relatives of somebody in this room. Drugs is like getting up and having a cup of tea in the morning."

A similarly furious reaction greeted Gallagher's comments, but he simply replied: "If by saying a few seemingly outrageous things has helped to instigate an open and honest debate about drug abuse in this country then I'm pleased."

Brian Harvey's career never fully recovered, and a few years later his ex-girlfriend Danniella Westbrook was involved in a drug scandal of her own (see overleaf).

# DANNIELLA WESTBROOK

Actress Danniella Westbrook entered the world of show business at a young age, appearing in commercials, musicals and children's dramas from the age of seven. Despite her butter-wouldn't-melt image, she first tried cocaine at 14 and ultimately became the public face of the drug's ravaging effects.

Westbrook's big break came in 1990 when she secured the part of Sam Mitchell in British soap *EastEnders*, quitting the show three years later to try her hand at new roles. The popularity of the Mitchell clan ensured that the show's producers were quick to ask her

back, and in 1995 Sam Mitchell returned to the screen. Regrettably, Westbrook had developed a major cocaine habit in the interim and was becoming unreliable on set. Poor timekeeping and erratic behaviour led to the termination of her contract the following year, but in 1999 she was given a third chance at stardom.

Westbrook was still in the grip of an addiction that was causing her septum to disintegrate, and in 2000 she was once again asked to leave the show. The same year, a shocking tabloid shot revealed the true extent of the damage to her nose, but even this failed to jolt the actress into sobriety. She finally entered rehab in 2002 after an incoherent appearance on *The Priory*, a now-defunct chat show. The role of Sam Mitchell was subsequently handed to actress Kim Medcalf.

Westbrook has since undergone extensive reconstructive work on her nose and revealed

the true extent of her addiction in her autobiography. She estimates that she spent over £250,000 on drugs, and admits that even pregnancy did not stop her from using. She later said, "I think there should be someone at *EastEnders* to say to young people when they come in, 'Look, your life is about to change, you're going to be invited to things, and you'll be offered drugs.' Someone who can tell them what sort of people are about, and what sort of papers, and how quickly what you've worked for all those years can be gone."

In 2009, Westbrook was invited to reprise the role of Sam Mitchell for a third time.

THINK THERE SHOULD BE SOMEONE AT EASTENDERS TO SAY TO YOUNG PEOPLE WHEN THEY COME IN, 'LOOK, YOUR LIFE IS ABOUT TO CHANGE, YOU'RE GOING TO BE INVITED TO THINGS, AND YOU'LL BE OFFERED DRUGS.'"

DANNIELLA WESTBROOK

WORDS OF WISDOM

"HAPPY IS HE WHO CAUSES A SCANDAL."

SALVADOR DALI

# A WEB
# OF LIES

"ALL ISSUES ARE POLITICAL
ISSUES, AND POLITICS
ITSELF IS A MASS OF LIES,
EVASIONS, FOLLY, HATRED
AND SCHIZOPHRENIA."

GEORGE ORWELL

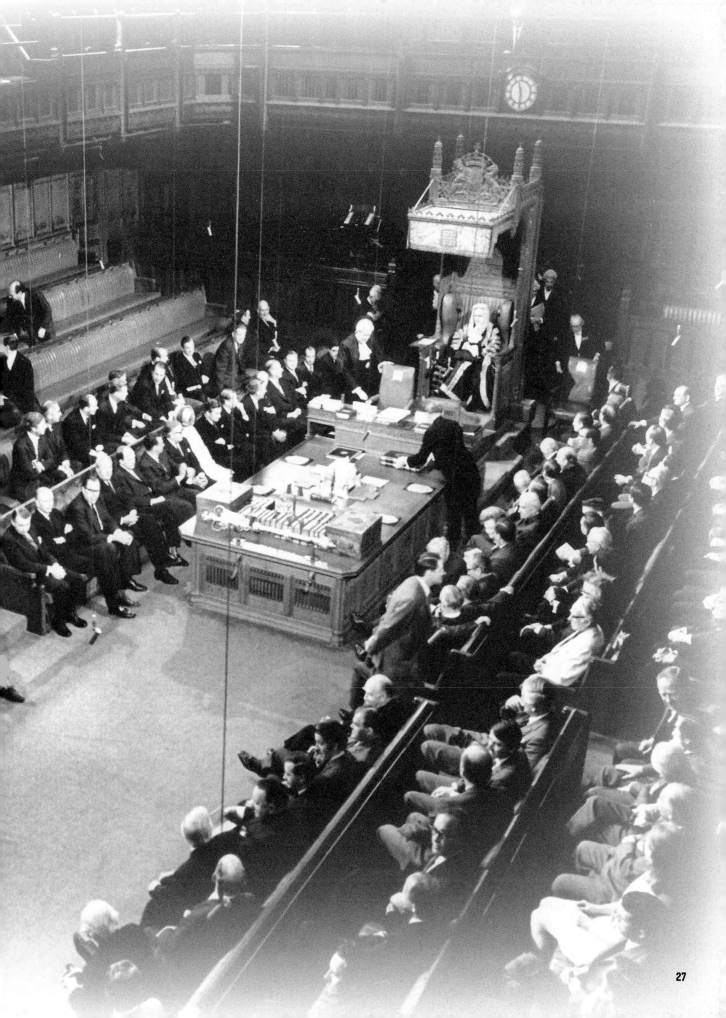

# RASPUTIN

Grigory Rasputin was born into humble beginnings in the late 1860s, growing up a semi-literate peasant in the Siberian village of Pokrovskoye. In spite of his impoverished background, he went on to become one of Russia's most controversial figures, the mystical "mad monk" with a dangerous influence over Tsar Nicholas II and his wife Tsaritsa Alexandra. Rasputin's monarchical-meddling and questionable sexual proclivities made him a notorious figure during the First World War, eventually resulting in a host of enduring myths about his self-proclaimed powers and bizarre assassination.

As a young man, Rasputin was said to have displayed supernatural powers, as well as experiencing visions of the Mother of God. The combined power of these events set him on the path of religious mysticism, and he later acted on these feelings by going on various pilgrimages. He eventually returned to Russia and developed quite a reputation – not just for his supposed healing powers, but also for his alleged links to the Khlysts, an orgiastic sect who believed

that exhaustion through sex was an acceptable means of communicating with God.

With a little help from Rasputin himself, word of his abilities began to spread. In 1905 he was called upon to "treat" Tsarevich Alexei, the haemophiliac son of Nicholas II and Alexandra. Rasputin succeeded where many doctors had failed, alleviating Alexei's symptoms and worming his way into the affections of Alexandra and Nicholas as a result. He continued to help in this way for many years, though it has since been suggested that he simply used hypnosis on Alexei, a stress-relieving technique occasionally seen to reduce the symptoms of haemophilia.

Rasputin's close association with the Tsar and his wife was a major cause for concern. The Russian Orthodox Church did not approve of his debauched reputation – nor his carousing and philandering, Rasputin reportedly eschewed basic hygiene – and the government feared he was giving unpatriotic advice to Nicholas. There were also rumours that Rasputin was having an affair with Alexandra and, thanks to Alexandra's German lineage, that both of them were acting as spies for Germany. On top of all this, the Russian public were wary of Rasputin;

OFFICER'S TRAGIC DEATH.

MYSTERY OF THE DEATH OF THE RUSSIAN MONK RASPUTIN.

Lieutenant and Quartermaster William Frederick Watterson, of the R.A.M.C., who was found dead at Aldershot with his head battered in. A sergeant was remanded yesterday in connection with the affair.

Prince Youssoupoff and his wife, a niece of the Tsar.

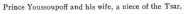

Prince Youssoupoff's name is being associated with the death of the monk Rasputin, who, it is said, was killed at the Petrograd house of one of the most aristocratic families in Russia. The body was afterwards thrown into the Neva, from which it was recovered. The Prince is well known in London and was at Oxford.

Rasputin, a most sinister personage.

# HOW I KILLED RASPUTIN THE MONK

## *Prince Tells of Poison, Shots and Blows*

### "HE WAS A DANGER TO MY COUNTRY"

Prince Felix Youssoupoff of Russia told an amazing story in the law courts yesterday of how he killed the monk Rasputin, the "evil genius" of Russia in the war.

"I induced him to go into a cellar under my palace in St. Petersburg," he said. "He ate cake and wine which contained poison sufficient to kill many men.

"At first it had little effect. . . . Then I shot him. He appeared to come to life again. . . . A fellow conspirator fired three shots at him. . . . He was still alive. I struck him with a loaded stick. . . . His body was thrown into the river."

While this grim tragedy was being enacted, music was being played in a room above the cellar, where three of the Prince's friends were sitting!

In the action, which is being heard before Mr. Justice Avory and a special jury, Princess Youssoupoff claims damages for alleged libel by the Metro-Goldwyn Mayer Pictures, Limited.

She complains that in the film "Rasputin, the Mad Monk," the character of Princess Natasha was portrayed in such a manner that it must inevitably be taken for her.

Sir William Jowitt, K.C., for the defence, surprised the Court by suggesting that it was the Grand Duke Dimitri, and not Prince Youssoupoff, who killed Rasputin.

The film character of Chegodieff, he said, represented the Grand Duke Dimitri; therefore the character of Natasha could not represent Princess Youssoupoff.

When the hearing was adjourned till to-day Prince Youssoupoff was still under cross-examination.

### PRINCE IN BOX

Prince Youssoupoff said he formerly lived at the Youssoupoff Palace on the Moika River, St. Petersburg.

In 1916 he made it his business to become acquainted with Rasputin, who told him something of his motives and objects, and of his ability to cure the young Tsarevitch.

Sir Patrick Hastings: Did he tell you the reasons why he was associated with Germany

#### WHO'S WHO IN THE CASE

**Princess Irena Alexandrovna Youssoupoff**, a niece and a second cousin of the murdered Tsar of Russia, is the plaintiff. She is the wife of

**Prince Youssoupoff**, a once-rich Russian, who now lives in Paris, and who admits that he killed

**Rasputin**, the unholy "monk," who gained tremendous power in 1914 over the Tsar and Tsarina of Russia because of his "ability to kill or cure" their young and ailing son, the Tsarevitch, by giving or withholding certain drugs of which he alone knew the secret.

and what he was doing in Russia for Germany? — Yes.

Leading up to the abdication of the Tsar and to Rasputin becoming the Lord or Tyrant of Russia? — Yes.

In consequence did you determine that Rasputin in the interests of your country should die? — Yes. Because I thought he was a danger for my country.

The Prince related how on the night of December 16 Rasputin, at his request, went to the Moika Palace.

A doctor had provided witness with poison for the purpose of assassinating Rasputin. It was to be administered in cakes and wine. Into what room did Rasputin go? — Into the cellar underground.

While he was there was there any music in the palace? — Yes. In my sitting-room above Who went into the cellar with Rasputin? — Myself. Anybody else at first? — No.

Was Rasputin supplied with the poisoned cakes and wine? — Yes. By me.

(Continued on page 4)

Prince and Princess Youssoupoff before leaving for yesterday's hearing of the case.

### ACCOLADE FOR ACTOR KNIGHT

Cedric Hardwicke, the well-known actor, accompanied by his wife (Helena Pickard), leaving home for Buckingham Palace yesterday, when he received the honour of knighthood.

**TO MARRY EARL'S BROTHER.** — Miss Barbara Frampton, whose engagement to the Hon. Edward Child-Villiers, brother of the Earl of Jersey and heir-presumptive to the title, is announced.

---

they did not know of Alexei's condition, or that Rasputin was treating it, and therefore grew suspicious of this former peasant and his growing influence on their country.

While the Tsar went to war for two years, Rasputin's grip on Alexandra – and potentially Russia – grew. He persuaded her to place his allies in important official roles, and offered disastrous advice on domestic matters. Meanwhile, Nicholas was away and unaware that his dynasty was in terminal decline. Anti-Rasputin feeling reached an all-time high, culminating in the assertion from politician Vladimir Purishkevich that Russia's ministers were now little more than Rasputin's puppets.

Prince Felix Yusupov and the Grand Duke

# AT THE GRAVE OF THE MONK RASPUTIN.

Dmitri Pavlovich agreed, and the trio plotted to kill Rasputin in December 1916. Having ensnared their victim in the basement of Yusupov's Moika Palace, they fed him red wine and cakes laced with cyanide. Amazingly, Rasputin was unaffected by the poison, prompting Yusupov to shoot him in the back. The men left him to die, but Yusupov returned to check the body. At this point Rasputin is said to have grabbed the Prince by the throat, only to have been shot several more times by Pavlovich and Purishkevich.

Determined that he would not survive, the conspirators clubbed Rasputin and threw him through an ice-hole in the frozen Neva river. When the body was eventually recovered, legend has it that the hands were raised, leading to suggestions that Rasputin had been trying to claw his way out of the ice. Unbelievably, the tale of his protracted death does not end here

– during cremation, Rasputin appeared to "sit up" in the flames, though this has since been attributed to improper preparation; the tendons were not snapped before cremation, causing them to bend in the heat and "raise" the body.

Rasputin was finally gone, but Russia's problems did not come to an end. The devastation of its military during the First World War could not be blamed on the "mad monk" after all, and Tsar Nicholas II was overthrown two months after Rasputin's death.

Many theories have arisen in regard to Rasputin's death. One is that the cyanide was rendered useless after being baked. Another extravagant claim is that Yusupov was in love with Rasputin and intentionally failed to kill him, going on to create the story of his apparent resurrection in order to hide his actions. Later forensic reports state that

Rasputin was shot four times, and that the third bullet went directly through his forehead, killing him instantly. The fatal bullet is said to have come from a British gun, though the only British officer known to have been in Russia at the time with that model of bullet has since taken the answer to his grave. It has been revealed, however, that British intelligence was deeply concerned by Rasputin's influence, as he appeared to be ousting pro-British ministers from the Russian cabinet. A further cause of concern was that Rasputin believed Russian troops should be withdrawn from battle; had this been acted on the German army would have been able to regroup and outnumber the allies.

RASPUTIN FILM.—Rasputin, the mysterious figure of pre-revolution Russia, receives a present from his old peasant friends. A scene from the film drama, "Rasputin," which is to be shown at the Plaza next week.

# RASPUTIN TRIVIA

- In 2005, rocker Ozzy Osbourne announced plans for a musical based on Rasputin's life. "He's like the original rock star," explained Ozzy. "I said to myself, 'What better thing to write about?'" The musical failed to materialize.
- Rasputin's penis is supposedly among the exhibits at St Petersburg's Erotica Museum, though its origin has never been verified. It is 11.8 inches long.
- Boney M's 'Ra Ra Rasputin' asserts that Rasputin was popular with "Moscow chicks", even though St Petersburg was Russia's capital at the time.

# THE CAMBRIDGE SPY RING

1950s Britain was outraged to learn that a home-grown spy ring had leaked information to the Soviet Union during the Second World War. Here's how it happened …

While studying at Cambridge, students Kim Philby, Donald Maclean, Guy Burgess and Anthony Blunt became staunch Communists, an ideological standpoint that resulted in their clandestine recruitment by the Soviets. Their less-than-patriotic exploits were exposed in 1951 after Washington-based Philby learned that US and British intelligence suspected Maclean of being a mole.

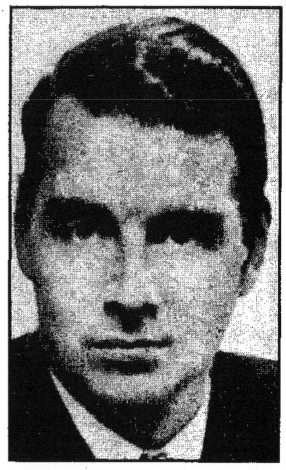

**BURGESS** *His friends in Moscow said yesterday that he was now on holiday.*

# Daily Mirror

3d.  Thursday, April 19, 1962  ✦  ✦  ✦  No. 18,144

# BURGESS AND MACLEAN ARREST RIDDLE

# BLUNT
# MY TREACHERY

**MACLEAN** He was in his flat in Moscow yesterday. He had "nothing to say."

Realizing he had to act fast before all of them were exposed, Philby immediately dispatched Burgess to inform Maclean, and the pair quickly left the UK. Philby's own activities were also now under suspicion, and he resigned from the Secret Intelligence Service after it became apparent that his future within the organization was far from assured. Philby eventually confessed, despite staging a press conference, during which he denied any involvement with such covert activities.

Blunt's role was not exposed until 1979, when investigative journalist Andrew Boyle branded him the "fourth man", and later that year Prime

# 'THIRD MAN' PHILBY—A NEW MI5 SHOCK

# PHILBY THE MASTER SPY—BY HIS SON

By BRIAN McCONNELL

## Are they flying in from Moscow?

Minister Margaret Thatcher sensationally revealed that Blunt had confessed all some 15 years earlier in return for immunity.

It has also been suggested that a fifth man existed, though his identity has never been settled upon.

### By BRIAN McCONNELL

**J**OHN PHILBY, son of the master spy Harold "Kim" Philby, who shook the West's counter-espionage system to the core, gave me exclusively last night the first full newspaper interview about his father.

Back in London after a trip to Moscow to see his father—who served the East, pretended to serve the West, and then defected to Russia—John said:

"He is now working there as a journalist, free for the first time in thirty-four years to think and speak freely, and being rewarded excellently for those many years' service to Communism."

Kim Philby was named as The Third Man in the Burgess and Maclean affair four

# Russia's reward: He is now a VIP

years after the two spies defected in 1951.

John, a former art student, now a freelance photographer, of Denning-road, Hampstead, was sent to Moscow to deliver a letter for The Sunday Times and to take pictures.

One of the pictures he took is shown on the left.

## Served

Although he had previously told radio and T V listeners that he did not talk to his father about his career as a spy, he told me last night:

"I am absolutely convinced —and it is obvious—that he is a Communist, has served

Communism of Soviet Russia for thirty-four years, ever since he left Cambridge in 1933.

"My sympathies are with him.

"I admire him very much, and although I do not disapprove of what he has done. I know he did not enjoy abusing his position or his friendships as a spy.

"What he did was for ideological reasons. He worked for thirty years without receiving anything for it.

"When I saw him in Moscow, he was being treated excellently, as one would expect to be treated for that service, a very important person, a VIP"

John added: "I spoke to him on two levels—on the level of a personal nature and on the level of someone from the Sunday Times.

How did the son, a Hampstead ratepayer, regard the father, a self-confessed double agent, who vanished in Beirut four years ago?

John said: "I was surprised to find that he had the strength and willpower to spend the greater part of his life as a double agent, but I can come to no other conclusion.

"He was a spy all that time—and I did not know it.

"Obviously he could not be where he is if he had

# The man in Moscow and the boy in London

*John Philby . . . back in London last night with the story of how his father shook the West.*

◆ **Continued on Back Page**

CENTURY OF SCANDAL A WEB OF LIES

# THE PROFUMO AFFAIR

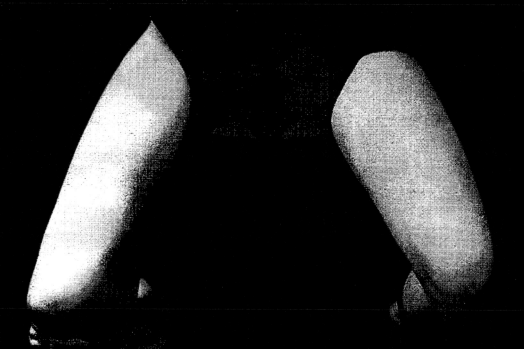

ABOVE: Christine Keeler.

The Profumo Affair was a 1963 scandal that rocked Harold Macmillan's Conservative government and destroyed the career of Secretary of State for War John Profumo. Profumo's actions were said to have threatened national security, and interest in the matter reverberated for so long that the story was eventually adapted for the big screen in 1989's *Scandal*.

John Profumo was a well-respected MP of considerable pedigree. He was educated at Harrow and Oxford and went on to serve with the British Army, most notably during the D-Day landings in Normandy. In 1940, a 25-year-old Profumo was elected to the House of Commons as Conservative MP for Kettering,

making him the youngest MP of the time. His public school connections and impressive war record ensured a steady rise through the Conservative ranks, where he held a number of junior positions before becoming Secretary of State for War in 1960.

The following year, Profumo attended a party thrown at Cliveden mansion by his friend Viscount Astor. It was here that he was introduced to 18-year-old Christine Keeler, a high-class call girl with whom he embarked on a brief affair. The liaison turned out to be disastrous despite only lasting a matter of weeks.

The veil of secrecy drawn over their union began to slip the following year. A shooting involving two of Keeler's acquaintances

**ABOVE:** Harold Macmillan.

had resulted in a police investigation of her activities, and the enquiry soon revealed the identity of her high-profile clients. Profumo was not publicly named, but rumours began to circulate – and what happened next made it impossible to hide his secret any longer.

The investigation into Keeler had also exposed her association with Russian naval attaché Yevgeny Ivanov, and rumours of her simultaneous relations with British MPs sparked fears that national security could have been breached. In early 1963, Profumo

was published in September 1963, one month before Harold Macmillan resigned. He cited ill-health for his departure, though many believed the stress of the Profumo Affair had finally taken its toll.

Although his political career was over, Profumo's marriage survived and he redeemed himself with years of volunteering and fundraising work for East London charity Toynbee Hall. His efforts were rewarded in 1975 when he was awarded a CBE, and in 1995 he sat next to the Queen at Margaret Thatcher's 70th birthday party. Thatcher later said, "It's time to forget the Keeler business. His has been a very good life," and went on to describe him as "one of our national heroes". Profumo maintained his silence on the affair for the rest of his life, even when press interest was reignited around

was forced to admit in parliament that he knew Keeler, but he lied by saying there was "no impropriety" in their relationship. This admission became front-page news and was rapidly turning into a major scandal, forcing Prime Minister Macmillan to step in and question Profumo. Despite assuring Macmillan that he was innocent of any wrongdoing, evidence emerged that painted Profumo as a liar, and he was forced to resign in disgrace. As it transpired, there was no substance to the claim that national security had been threatened, but Profumo's worst crime appeared to have been his dishonesty.

A government investigation into the incident

**ABOVE:** John
Profumo with
his wife Valerie
Hobson.

**RIGHT:** Christine
Keeler.

the release of *Scandal*. He died aged 91 after
suffering a stroke in 2006.

Keeler was imprisoned for nine months
in December 1963 after being found guilty of
perjury in relation to a separate court case.
At the height of the Profumo Affair, she posed
nude – sitting on a backwards-facing chair
to preserve her modesty – to promote a film
entitled *The Keeler Affair*. Although the film
was not released in Britain, the photograph
was reprinted countless times and went on to
become an iconic image of the 1960s. She was

also involved with the making of *Scandal* and later released a book detailing her version of the Profumo Affair. Keeler has intimated that there are still many truths to be revealed, but official documents pertaining to the affair cannot be opened until 2046.

"WHAT DID THE PRESIDENT KNOW AND WHEN DID HE KNOW IT?"

QUESTION BY SENATOR HOWARD BAKER DURING THE WATERGATE SENATE HEARINGS

# WATERGATE

Watergate was a major political scandal of the 1970s that resulted in Richard Nixon becoming the first and only US president to resign from office. Its impact was so great that the "-*gate*" suffix has since entered the English language as a common tool for describing social and political scandals. Read on to discover how a seemingly straightforward burglary case turned into a political nightmare that gripped America for years.

On 17th June 1972, five men with photographic equipment and bugging devices were arrested for breaking into the headquarters of the Democratic National Committee, located on the sixth floor of the Watergate Hotel in Washington DC. They were caught rifling through confidential papers and bugging the office of Nixon's political opponents, actions that would eventually trigger a national crisis.

Relying heavily on anonymous sources, *Washington Post* reporters Bob Woodward and Carl Bernstein famously linked the burglars to the 1972 Committee to Re-elect the President. They also uncovered information indicating that Nixon's administration were aware of the break-in, and determined to silence any coverage of it. Investigations into the FBI, CIA and even the White House followed. One of their anonymous sources was nicknamed Deep Throat after the outrageous 1970s porn film of the same name; he managed to keep his identity hidden until 2005 when he outed himself in a *Vanity Fair*

interview as former Deputy Director of the FBI, William Mark Felt Sr.

The trial didn't end with the conviction of the burglars, however – as the media spotlight increased, so did the investigations. A senate committee was set up to examine Watergate and it began issuing subpoenas to White House staff members.

President Nixon's staff conspired to cover up the break-in, but a series of court battles revealed that surveillance systems in Nixon's office had recorded all calls and conversations to have taken place there. Since some of these were related to the burglary, the US Supreme Court demanded Nixon hand the tapes over. Media coverage of the break-in and re-election campaign was huge, and as publicity increased, so did the repercussions of the actions of Nixon's administration.

# NIXON IN DANGER

*Nixon—storm over tapes.*

From RALPH CHAMPION and MARK DOWDNEY in New York

**P**RESIDENT NIXON was facing the grave peril of impeachment last night as the Watergate scandal exploded once again.

At least four Democratic Congressmen threatened to take impeachment action—which, if successful, would mean Nixon's expulsion from office.

Waves of protest swept America after a 24-hour drama in which Nixon took drastic steps to prevent his private White House tape-recordings being handed over to a court.

First he ordered Attorney-General Elliot Richardson to sack special Watergate prosecutor Archibald Cox. But Richardson refused, and resigned.

Then Nixon told Richardson's deputy William Ruckelshaus to fire Cox.

Ruckelshaus also refused — and was sacked himself by Nixon.

**Armed**

Finally, Nixon appointed Solicitor-General Robert Bork, a right-wing law professor, as acting Attorney-General. And it was Bork who sacked Cox. Cox's whole department of ninety young lawyers was shut down. Armed FBI agents were sent into prevent them entering their offices.

The lawyers were even refused permission to collect personal photographs and love letters.

Cox's chief deputy, Henry Ruth, said: "I thought this

could never happen. I never thought an FBI agent could tell me I must not take home a love letter from my wife."

Last night there was a suggestion that there might be mass resignations from the Justice Department in protest against Nixon's action.

Republican Congressman John Anderson said yesterday: "The President has acted irresponsibly, and has precipitated a constitutional crisis.

"He added: 'Impeachment resolutions will be raining down like hailstones.'"

The storm broke last Friday when Nixon offered a compromise in the bitter legal battle for the White House tapes.

He had been ordered by an appeal court to hand over the tapes to a judge to decide whether they were relevant to the Watergate affair.

Nixon could have taken the case to the Supreme Court. Instead, he offered to provide the Senate investigating committee and Cox with a personally-selected summary of the tapes.

These would have been vouched for by one of Nixon's old friends, 72-year-old Senator John Stennis.

Cox rejected the offer, leading to the confrontation between himself and Richardson on one side and Nixon on the other.

Nixon claimed that the Senate committee, headed by Senator Sam Ervin, had accepted the offer. But even this was not certain last night.

Cox had been conducting a separate Grand Jury inquiry.

## Impeachment move follows sackings in new Watergate row

Continued on Page Two

# NIXON IN NEW COVER-UP ROW

### From MARK DOWDNEY
### In New York

**P**RESIDENT NIXON has decided NOT to publish the Watergate tapes for fear that they may implicate him in the cover-up scandal.

The move marks a breakdown in Operation Candour — the President's campaign to convince Americans that he has nothing to hide.

Nixon made his decision to hang on to the tapes after a top-level meeting with his aides in the White House on Boxing Day. They told him that after listening to

## He decides not to release the tapes

the tapes for several weeks, they had concluded that the recordings could damage the President's image.

Nixon has always claimed that it was March 21 before he learned that his aides were covering-up after the break-in at Democratic Party headquarters.

But the tapes apparently show that he knew several days before—a disclosure which could convince many people that he not only knew about the cover-up, but that he took part in it.

Another problem with the tapes,

according to White House aides, is that they are full of presidential swear words and show Nixon's concern for "petty" political revenge against people who annoy him.

"There are a lot of really nasty comments about individuals," says one White House aide.

It was disclosed yesterday that Nixon is helping former aides Bob Haldeman and John Ehrlichman to defend themselves against criminal charges arising out of the Watergate affair.

Copies of all the White House documents and papers turned over to the Watergate special prosecutor are being secretly sent to their lawyer.

This contrasts with the White House's refusal to allow other former aides, like John Dean and Egil Krogh, to consult their old files for the same purpose.

---

Below is a timeline of the Watergate scandal.

## CHRONOLOGY OF EVENTS

### 5th November 1968

Republican nominee Richard Nixon wins the 1968 presidential election over Democrat nominee Hubert Humphrey. His campaign promises to restore "law and order".

### 21st January 1969

Nixon inaugurated as 37th President of the United States.

### 17th June 1972

Five men with bugging devices are arrested for breaking into the headquarters of the Democratic National Committee within the Watergate complex. Dubbed "The White House Plumbers" because of their ability to prevent sensitive information from "leaking":

their names are Bernard L Barker, Virgilio R Gonzalez, Eugenio R Martinez, James W McCord Jr and Frank A Sturgis.

### 15th September 1972

A grand jury indicts the Plumbers and two others (E Howard Hunt Jr and G Gordon Liddy) for conspiracy, burglary and violation of federal wiretapping laws.

### 10th October 1972

FBI agents determine that the men connected to the Watergate break-in are also connected to the Committee to Re-elect the President.

### 7th November 1972

In a landslide victory, President Nixon secures a second term in office.

### 30th January 1973

The Plumbers are tried and convicted. Trial

judge John J Sirica suspects a conspiracy involving senior government officials. Watergate is subsequently investigated further by the Senate Watergate Committee, House Judiciary Committee and the media. Members of White House staff are issued with subpoenas ordering them to examine Watergate.

## March 1973

James McCord writes a letter to Sirica, claiming he was under political pressure to plead guilty. In doing so, he implicates high-ranking government officials including former Attorney General John Mitchell. His letter raises the profile of Watergate.

## 30th April 1973

The scandal causes senior White House staffers H R Haldeman, John Ehrlichman and Attorney General Richard Kleindienst to resign. Nixon fires White House Counsel John Dean, who had just testified before the Senate and went on to become a key witness against President Nixon (see 3rd June 1973).

## 18th May (to August 7th) 1973

Senate Watergate Committee hearings begin. They are broadcast, causing major political damage to the President. An estimated 85% of Americans with television sets tune in to at least one portion of the hearings.

## 3rd June 1973

John Dean tells investigators that he and Nixon discussed the cover-up on more than 30 occasions.

## 13th June 1973

It is revealed by former Presidential Appoints

# NIXON ON THE BRINK

Nixon . . . harried and on the run.

**H**IS political career was in ruins, smashed by a disastrous election defeat. And he announced the death of his ambition bitterly and ungraciously.

"You won't have Richard Nixon to kick around any more," he snarled at America.

That was nine years ago. His first fall after a dazzling rise through Washington's corridors of power.

Now they're kicking Richard Nixon around again—and harder than he ever dreamed possible.

On the steps of the White House, grim-faced lawyers hand over the historic subpoenas that lay down the battle lines.

Up on Capitol Hill, the Watergate committee and the world listen to the sickening daily catalogue of corruption and arrogant criminality perpetrated in his name.

**And suddenly, Richard Milhous Nixon is on the brink of his second fall.**

It would all have been unthinkable, even as a mind-exercising scenario, a mere six months ago.

**DAVID WRIGHT reports from Washington**

## Triumph

Then, wearing morning coat and a fixed smile, the President rode in triumph to his second inauguration after being swept back into office with one of the biggest majorities ever.

He was about to end the Vietnam war and convince the nation he was bringing American troops and prisoners of war home "with honour."

The public admiration for his "voyages of peace" to Peking and Moscow still lingered.

And 75 per cent. of the American people told an opinion poll they had either never heard of Watergate—or didn't care.

Only six months ago . . . but so different now.

Nixon, harried and on the run, is shut away in the oval office of the White House, preparing for what could be his last battle over the legal and constitutional issues raised by his refusal to hand over the White House tapes.

His life has been a fascinating mixture of dizzy success and crashing, bone-jarring failure since 1946.

It was then that he left the U S Navy, made the first political speech of his life, and left California for the House of Representatives in Washington.

Within two years he had made his name by taking a leading role in — Ironically — the Watergate-style pursuit of Alger Hiss, a former State Department official accused of un-American activities.

By 1950 he was ready for the

U S Senate, and won his second election easily amid accusations of unfair tactics.

At 39, he became the second youngest Vice-President in history.

He served two terms under Ike, and won the respect of Nikita Kruschev.

As far as America was concerned, it seemed to be next stop the Presidency for Nixon.

But a young Senator called John F. Kennedy turned that dream into a nightmare for the California shopkeeper's son.

Kennedy threw his magnetism and wealth into the 1960 campaign. Nixon lost vital television debates, then the election, to him.

Two years later he was defeated in the race for the Governorship of California.

It seemed inconceivable that he could rise from the political ashes.

## Murky

But there he was in 1968, coming back to snatch the Presidency from Hubert Humphrey.

Nixon was on top again, and this time seemed to stay there . . . until the murky tides of Watergate finally began lapping at the doors of the White House.

He has ruled out resignation, but the talk of the once-unthinkable—impeachment—grows every day.

Whatever the outcome of the fight over the tapes that could clear or convict him, it will be a tough and bloody one.

For Nixon has never forgotten the advice of his football coach at college.

"There were no excuses for failure," Nixon says. "He didn't feel sorry for you when you got knocked down."

The coach also had an unusual definition of being a good loser.

According to Nixon, he used to say: "You know what a good loser is?

"It's somebody who HATES to lose."

# "I AM NOT A CROOK."

## PRESIDENT RICHARD NIXON

# President says: I'll hand over Watergate tapes

Secretary Alexander Butterfield that recording equipment in Nixon's office had been taping all calls and conversations since 1971.

## 23rd July 1973

Nixon refuses to release the tapes, citing his executive privilege as President of the United States.

## 20th October 1973

Nixon fires the Special Prosecutor, a move that causes Attorney General Richardson and Deputy Attorney General William Ruckelshaus to resign. These events are later referred to as "The Saturday Night Massacre".

## 17th November 1973

Nixon famously insists, "I'm not a crook".

## 7th December 1973

An unexplained 18-minute gap is found in a subpoenaed tape recorded three days after the Watergate break-in (see 4th August 1974).

## 1st March 1974

Dubbed the "Watergate Seven", former presidential aides Haldeman, Ehrlichman, Mitchell, Charles Colson, Gordon C Strachan, Robert Mardian and Kenneth Parkinson are indicted for conspiring to hinder the Watergate investigation. The grand jury secretly names Nixon as an unindicted co-conspirator.

## 5th April 1974

Former Nixon Appointments Secretary Dwight Chapin is convicted of lying to the grand jury.

## 24th July 1974

In the *United States v. Nixon* case, the Supreme Court rules that Nixon must hand over recordings of 64 White House conversations. He complies.

## 27th July 1974

The House Judiciary Committee votes in favour of impeaching Nixon, citing his "misuse of government agencies" during the Watergate cover-up.

## 4th August 1974

The tape recorded on 23rd June 1972 is finally released. Recorded shortly after the break-in, it documents Nixon and Haldeman formulating a plan to block the Watergate investigations. It becomes clear that Nixon knew of the involvement of White House officials and the Campaign for the Re-election of the President. The tape becomes known as "The smoking gun", and seals Nixon's fate.

# NIXON GIVES IN

## 8th August 1974

Nixon resigns. In a broadcast to millions on television and radio, he admits:

"I would have preferred to carry through to the finish, whatever the personal agony it would have involved, and my family unanimously urged me to do so. But the interest of the Nation must always come before any personal considerations.

"From the discussions I have had with Congressional and other leaders, I have concluded that because of the Watergate matter I might not have the support of the Congress that I would consider necessary to back the very difficult decisions and carry out the duties of this office in the way the interests of the Nation would require.

"I have never been a quitter. To leave office before my term is completed is abhorrent to every instinct in my body. But as President, I must put the interest of America first. America needs a full-time President and a full-time Congress, particularly at this time with problems we face at home and abroad.

"To continue to fight through the months ahead for my personal vindication would almost totally absorb the time and attention of both the President and the Congress in a period when our entire focus should be on the great issues of peace abroad and prosperity without inflation at home.

"Therefore, I shall resign the Presidency

# "A serious act of omission which I deeply regret"

# NIXON PLAYS HIS LAST CARD

effective at noon tomorrow. Vice President [Gerald] Ford will be sworn in as President at that hour in this office."

## 8th September 1974

Controversially, President Ford ends the Watergate investigations, granting Nixon a pardon.

## 22nd April 1994

Richard Nixon dies. He remains a divisive figure, albeit one eulogized in hindsight by the political establishment.

## 21st May 2005

W Mark Felt Sr, former Associate Director of the FBI during the Watergate era, reveals to *Vanity Fair* that he is Deep Throat.

## 18th December 2008

W Mark Felt Sr dies at the age of 95.

Watergate continues to attract conspiracy theories and remains a talking point in popular culture. In 2007, *Frost/Nixon* attracted five Oscar nominations and won countless other awards. The film is based on Peter Morgan's dramatization of David Frost's 1977 grilling of Nixon.

# NIXON GETS OFF

## WORDS THAT DEFINED A SCANDAL

"I would say only that if some of my judgments were wrong, and some were wrong, they were made in what I believed at the time to be the best interest of the nation."
President Richard Nixon, announcing his intent to resign, 8th August 1974

"I assume the presidency under extraordinary circumstances... This is an hour of history that troubles our minds and hurts our hearts."
Gerald Ford when he took over after Nixon's resignation

"What distinctive quality of the presidency permits its incumbent to withhold evidence?"
Judge John J Sirica

"A third-rate burglary attempt."
Nixon's Press Secretary Ron Zeigler's first comment on Watergate

"This is the operative statement. The others are inoperative."
Ron Ziegle, Nixon's press secretary

# HITLER DIARIES

The world was intrigued when German magazine *Stern* announced it was to serialize Hitler's diaries in 1983 – a new insight into the Second World War was about to be revealed.

**DAILY MIRROR, Saturday, May 7, 1983**     **PAGE 7**

## ...THE SUNDAY TIMES

**WORLD EXCLUSIVE: How the diaries of the Fuehrer were found in an East German hayloft**

## The secrets of Hitler's war

—The Sunday Times front page two weeks ago

# The scoop that never was

*Stern* journalist Gerd Heidemann had apparently located the diaries in an East German barn, claiming they had remained there since 1945 after being retrieved from a crashed plane. The magazine paid $5 million for the books, while *The Sunday Times* parted with £400,000

# Hitler diaries exposed as fakes

Sure enough, the diaries were found to be a hoax, riddled with historical inaccuracies and printed on modern paper. Heidemann eventually confessed to buying the counterfeit texts from Konrad Kujau, a Stuttgart dealer in military relics. Both men were found guilty of fraud and forgery and sentenced to four and a half years in prison, though Kujau later established a successful business selling fake versions of famous paintings.

to secure British serialization rights. The discovery proved too good to be true, however: British historian Lord Dacre, brought in to authenticate the diaries, was having second thoughts. At a Hamburg press conference, he announced: "I must say I regret that the normal methods of historical verification have been sacrificed to the requirements of the journalistic scoop."

THE HITLER diaries were finally declared forgeries yesterday after tests were carried out on the paper, ink and binding of some of the 60 volumes.

After the announcement the West German government, the Sunday Times, which had bought British rights from the German magazine Stern, immediately said it would suspend publication of the series.

Rupert Murdoch, the Australian proprietor of the Sunday Times, said after flying into New York last night: "I'm very disappointed."

He added: "We hoped that we had got hold of the genuine thing. We thought we were running with it. It made some great Fleet Street rat-packery bang-bangery."

Mr Murdoch said that the Sunday Times chiefs had accepted the judgment of historian Lord Dacre, who at first believed the diaries to be genuine.

The newspaper boss went on: "We said to him, 'If there is as much as a two per cent chance of this being wrong, let us know.'

Stern, which claimed the diaries were found in an East German hayloft after a three-year search, also said it was stopping publication of the diaries.

"I DID NOT HAVE SEXUAL RELATIONS WITH THAT WOMAN."

BILL CLINTON

# BILL CLINTON AND MONICA LEWINSKY

During his eight years in office, America's 42nd President eliminated national debt, improved the economy and increased spending on education and welfare. When he left his position in 2001, he scored an approval rating of 66% – the highest end of career rating for any post-war president. This stamp of success could have been significantly lower were it not for the forgiving nature of the American public. They eventually overlooked Clinton's notorious

# CLINTON'S SEX FILES

SHAME: Clinton apologises again yesterday

- Bill fondled Monica's breasts
- They had oral sex nine times
- He used cigar in kinky game
- He called her Sweetie or Baby

THE world was in shock last night after President Bill Clinton's sex shame with Monica Lewinsky was laid bare.

In devastating detail over the worldwide web, the explosive Starr report claimed Clinton kissed and fondled Lewinsky's naked breasts, made genital contact

**From ANDY LINES and ROD CHAYTOR in Washington**

and took part in a bizarre sex act involving a cigar. The couple had oral sex NINE times.

The president called 24-year-old Lewinsky 'Sweetie,' 'Baby' and 'Dear' – and said the two of them were 'emotive and full of fire.'

Lewinsky called him

'Handsome' and thought they might one day wed.

Last night even some of Clinton's closest aides believed he could not survive.

Prosecutor Kenneth Starr's 445-page Zippergate dossier went out on the Internet claiming the fallen president had committed 11 acts for which he could be

TURN TO PAGE TWO

DREAM: Monica "thought she could be wife"

womanizing streak, a character trait which resulted in the famous Lewinsky scandal and his subsequent impeachment in 1998.

In July 1995, 22-year-old psychology graduate Monica Lewinsky accepted an unpaid internship at the White House. By the end of the year she had advanced surprisingly quickly to a paid position, and was spending increasing amounts of time with the President. This development did not go unnoticed, and for good reason – it later emerged the pair had been conducting an affair.

# HUMILIATED

NOV 17 1995

SEPT 21 1998

## Warning: Testimony may contain explicit details.

CLOSE: Lewinsky and Clinton at the White House in a picture released for the first time yesterday     TV TORMENT: How the world saw Clinton yesterday on the video of his Grand Jury testimony

## World sees Clinton shamed in video quiz

By ANDY LINES, US Editor, and ROD CHAYTOR in Washington

PRESIDENT Bill Clinton, humiliated in front of the world, was last night awaiting America's verdict on his dramatic trial by television.

Hundreds of millions across the globe watched yesterday as the most powerful man on earth squirmed through a grilling about his affair with Monica Lewinsky.

He was further rocked by documents giving more sordid details. New pictures were released showing Clinton's affection for the White House trainee.

But many White House aides were buoyant last night — believing the President had come through relatively unscathed and will survive attempts to drive him from office.

Prime Minister Tony Blair was at Clinton's side in New York as reaction to the video flooded in.

Never before has a President's shame been so openly paraded as on the tape of his testimony over the affair. Viewers were warned it contained explicit material. They saw Clinton being evasive and finally losing his temper.

He quibbled over legal definitions and at one point said: "I am not going to answer your trick questions."

As the tape of his Grand Jury

TURN TO PAGE 2

## PRESIDENT'S TRIAL ON TV: PAGES 2, 3, 4, 5, 6, 7, 8 & 9

Suspicious White House staff arranged for Lewinsky to be moved to a lower profile position at the Pentagon, somewhere she would be separated from Clinton. Despite the move, the affair continued on an irregular basis into early 1997, during which time a somewhat naive Lewinsky confessed her indiscretions to new friend and colleague Linda Tripp. Tripp appeared to have Lewinsky's best interests at heart, advising her young charge not to clean a blue dress that was stained with Clinton's semen – a piece of evidence that would later prove crucial. What Lewinsky didn't know, however, was that Tripp was also recording their intimate telephone conversations about the affair.

Clinton was already in hot water around this time – a former Arkansas state employee named Paula Jones was suing him for sexual harassment. Her case was dismissed, but when she appealed, Clinton settled out of court with a significant cash payment. During

SO GRAPHIC SO SORDID.. SO DAMNING

FIGHT: Clinton, left, yesterday, facing a new crisis

MONICAGATE
Listen to the tapes of the woman who brought President Clinton to his knees

# Rejected, humiliated.. Monica came to hit him where it hurts

## LEWINSKY TELLS GRAND JURY: PRESIDENT LIED

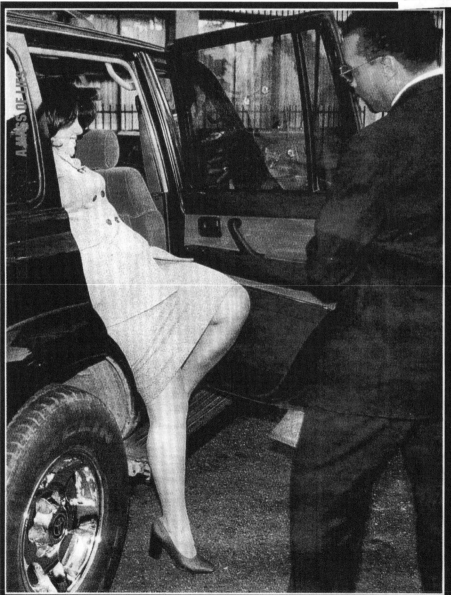

THE AVENGER: A security man greets Monica Lewinsky as she makes an ungainly arrival courthouse yesterday

SHOWDOWN: Lewinsky heads for her session with the jury

SO HURT: She's vowed to get her own back on the President

# CLINTON COMES CLEAN

## He will admit to sex act with Monica..but claim he never lied about the affair because they didn't go the whole way

the initial proceedings brought by Jones, Lewinsky was called to the stand where she denied under oath that she had been sexually involved with Clinton. Upon hearing this, Tripp exposed her lie by handing over the tapes she had secretly recorded.

Clinton later spoke on national television to assure America that he "did not have sexual relations with that woman, Miss Lewinsky," and attempted to convince a court he had not been lying when he told an aide there was nothing going on between him and Lewinsky. Many were astounded when he explained, "It depends on what the meaning of the word 'is' is… if 'is' means 'is and never has been,' that is one thing. If it means 'there is none,' that was a completely true statement… Now, if someone had asked me on that day, 'are you having any kind of sexual relations with Ms. Lewinsky,' that is, asked me a question in the present tense, I would have said no. And it would have been completely true."

Clinton finally admitted his "improper" conduct with Lewinsky after the blue dress was revealed but maintained he had not lied since his definition of sexual relations did not include oral sex – something Lewinsky admitted to performing on him in the Oval Office.

Unsurprisingly, this explanation was not satisfactory for some and Clinton was impeached on suspicion of perjury. This 21-day trial ended after the majority vote required to remove him failed to materialize. A shame-faced Clinton

was allowed to complete the end of his second and final term, but his reputation appeared to be irrevocably damaged – even the unwavering support of his wife Hillary did little to boost his public image. Lewinsky experienced a brief period of celebrity and later claimed that Clinton had been "revisionist" in the version of events recorded in his 2004 autobiography *My Life*.

Although the immediate aftermath of his impeachment was a bleak period for Clinton, time proved to be a healer. When he left office the general consensus among Americans appeared to be that he had done a great job, even if he was untrustworthy in his personal life. A 2007 Gallup poll saw him voted fourth greatest president in US history, and he is now said to earn millions from speaking engagements.

"I HAVE BEEN SILLY, VERY FOOLISH. WHAT ELSE CAN I SAY?"

JEFFREY ARCHER

# JEFFREY ARCHER

In 1986, author and former politician Jeffrey Archer was forced to resign as deputy chairman of the Conservative Party after a *News of the World* report that he had paid prostitute Monica Coghlan £2,000 to leave the UK. Archer claimed to have fallen victim to a sting, insisting he had never met Coghlan and had made a serious error of judgement in trying to make the matter disappear. When questioned as to why he had allowed himself to be conned, Archer replied: "I have been silly, very foolish. What else can I say?"

Meanwhile, the *Daily Star* echoed the story – but they went even further, alleging that Archer had indeed met

## 'ARCHER TRAPPED HIMSELF'

CENTURY OF SCANDAL A MASS OF LIES

# I WAS A FOOL

# ARCHER THE LEPER

Coghlan, and that the pair had slept together.

Archer successfully sued the *Star* and was awarded £500,000 in damages, but this 1987 victory was not the end of the story. In 1999, *News of the World* reported that Archer's friend Ted Francis had lied during the trial. The allegation forced then Conservative leader William Hague to suspend Archer for five years while a perjury investigation was launched, and in April 2000 police moved in as a result of the new allegations. Archer was found guilty of perjury and perverting the course of justice, receiving a four-year prison sentence and being ordered to pay £1.3 million in legal fees and reimburse the *Star*'s £500,000.

Although he only served half of his sentence, Archer was embroiled in another scandal during his time in prison. While staying in an "open" facility in Lancashire, he broke the rules of his curfew by attending a friend's party. The Prison Service branded his behaviour "a serious breach of trust" and moved him back to a closed prison as a result.

**RIGHT:** Jeffrey Archer and wife Mary.

# JOHN MAJOR AND EDWINA CURRIE

Although former Prime Minister John Major was regularly lampooned for being dull – his satirical *Spitting Image* puppet was completely grey – his former colleague Edwina Currie revealed in 2002 that they had conducted a four-year affair prior to his role as leader. Major, who had otherwise kept a low profile since stepping down as PM in 1997, was moved to issue the

# BLUE PANTS WILL COME CLEAN

## Major to face press

### EDWINA'S LOVE POEM..ROPEY AND SELF–OBSESSED AS ANY TEENAGER

*And oh, I weep for these things, in the dark fastnesses of the night*
*For my lost love*
*And for my lost hope*
*And for the future we are about to lose*
*And for all the incompetence and stupidity I witness and can do nothing about*
*And for all the pain*
*All the pain*
*Which still grieves me so*
*And for all the talent I don't have and can't share*
*And all the talent I don't have, to be a success elsewhere*
*And for those who love me, and can't meet my expectations, especially Ray and Debbie*
*And mostly for John, because he, too, let me down*
*- and is letting us all down*
*- by being too cautious*
*- by being too small-minded*
*- by obeying too many rules*
*I taught him*
*How to ignore rules*
*How to take risks*
*How to measure risk, and live with it, and love it - relish it, enjoy the edge we walk on; to fly…*

**OLIVER JAMES** Psychologist and author assesses it

EDWINA Currie wrote this extraordinary poem in the early hours of March 4, 1992 after 45 minutes alone with Major in his Downing Street flat.

It has all the self-obsession of a depressive teenager. The self-pity, the self-importance, the anger at being failed in a world where only they know what is right and everyone else is inadequate.

In teenagers such ropey thinking is common but in adults it is a sign of a personality disorder.

Such people are tremendously selfish, focused on their own feelings and thoughts, unable to realise the damage their behaviour does to others. We should feel sorry for her because, as her poem conveys all too clearly, she lives in a dreadfully unhappy place.

following statement:

"It is the one event in my life of which I am most ashamed and I have long feared would be made public."

He also confirmed that his wife Norma was aware of the indiscretion – which began in 1984 – and had subsequently forgiven him.

This was not Currie's first involvement in a scandal; as Junior Health Minister she remarked in 1988 that most of Britain's eggs were infected with salmonella. The ensuing storm saw egg sales plummet dramatically and eventually forced her to resign.

# THE INCREDIBLE AFFAIR

SCANDAL: Parkinson and Keays

# RIGHT COW

FROM PAGE ONE

October 1985, she said: "I feel very sorry for Cecil and his family.

"Most of my thoughts on Sara Keays are unprintable. Perhaps the most polite thing to say is she's a right cow."

Yesterday the comments came back to haunt Edwina as she continued to cash in on her sleazy past. Her kiss-and-tell diaries are said to be heading for the bestseller list.

But when Keays wrote a book about her relationship with Parkinson, Edwina was quick to criticise.

While other Tories kept silent as Keays revealed how she became the mother of Parkinson's love child Flora,

> 6 Take a look at his smelly socks, frayed shirt cuffs and full ashtray. If you fancy sorting that lot out, go for him 9
>
> EDWINA CURRIE, Oct 85

Edwina went on the attack. She also dished out words of advice to any would-be Sara Keays.

Edwina said: "Take a look at his smelly socks, frayed shirt-cuffs and full ashtray.

"If you fancy sorting that lot out then go for him."

On another occasion she was asked if she would be interested in a relationship with 80s heart-throb Simon Le Bon.

She replied: "He's married isn't he? That does stop some people from doing it, one would hope."

A Tory insider said last night: "Edwina wanted to be seen as the devoted wife who would not condone any kind of marital misbehaviour.

"It is now apparent that this was nothing more than a show. She may well regret making those comments now."

# ALEXANDER LITVINENKO

Industrial espionage is something most of us associate with James Bond films, but this mysterious underworld was made real when a London restaurant was contaminated with radioactive polonium in November 2006. Traces of the deadly substance were discovered in the Piccadilly branch of Itsu shortly after a patron named Alexander Litvinenko fell ill, and journalists were quick to discover his background in Russian intelligence.

The rapid deterioration of Litvinenko's health was attributed to poisoning by radionuclide polonium-210, leading to the immediate closure of Itsu. Much lower levels of polonium were also discovered on several aeroplanes, and passengers who had travelled on them were warned that their health could be at risk. Litvinenko died on 23rd November, aged 43. The poison took 22 days to kill him.

Litvinenko was a former officer of the Soviet KGB and Russian Federal Security Service, and had been granted asylum in England after his life was deemed to be at risk in Russia. He became a journalist and writer, publishing two books, *Blowing up Russia: Terror from within* and *Lubyanka Criminal Group*.

These highly controversial texts accused Russian secret services of bringing Vladimir Putin to power via terrorist acts, and even pointed the finger at Putin himself for the murder of Russian journalist Anna Politkovskaya. Litvinenko's widow would later make similar claims about Moscow's role in her husband's death, though she stopped short of directly naming Putin. She also stated that she could not cooperate with Russian authorities over fears they would misrepresent her evidence.

Although British police were quick to announce Andrey Lugovy, – a former officer of the Russian Federal Protective Service – as their top suspect, Russian authorities refused to hand him over. Nobody has been charged with Litvinenko's murder, but in July 2008 a British security source told the BBC: "We very strongly believe the Litvinenko case to have had some state involvement. There are very strong indications."

Litvinenko clearly agreed. In what would become his chilling final statement, the ailing Russian announced:

"This may be the time to say one or two things to the person responsible for my present condition. You may succeed in silencing me but that silence comes at a price. You have shown yourself to be as barbaric and ruthless as your most hostile critics have claimed. You have shown yourself to have no respect for life, liberty or any civilized value. You have shown yourself to be unworthy of your office, to be unworthy of the trust of civilized men and women. You may succeed in silencing one man but the howl of protest from around the world will reverberate, Mr Putin, in your ears for the rest of your life.

"May God forgive you for what you have done, not only to me but to beloved Russia and its people."

BELOW:
A hearse arrives at Highgate Cemetery, London, with the body of Alexander Litvinenko.

# SPY DIES

## 'The bastards got me'..last words of poisoned Russian

By ALLISON MARTIN and VANESSA ALLEN

POISONED ex-Russian spy Alexander Litvinenko died in hospital last night.

The former KGB officer, whose friends say he was targeted by Russian agents, declared hours before his death: "The bastards got me."

Litvinenko, 43, had been fighting for his life after having a heart attack. He was admitted to London's University College Hospital a week ago in a serious condition and was put under armed guard.

Police later said they believed he had been deliberately poisoned. Doctors and detectives were last night still carrying out tests to discover exactly what struck him down.

His friends insist he was poisoned because of his fierce criticism of President Putin's regime. The Kremlin has strenuously denied the accusations.

**FULL STORY: PAGE 9**

A hearse arrives at Highgate Cemetery, London, with the body of Alexander Litvinenko.

67

# THE MPs' EXPENSES SCANDAL

The UK's Parliamentary expenses scandal was a long time coming. A campaign to force government ministers to reveal their spending habits began as far back as January 2005, when the *Daily Telegraph* attempted to access the expenses receipts of six MPs.

The newspaper cited the Freedom of Information Act (FOIA) in its bid to retrieve the relevant data, but was controversially rebuffed by the Commons. This refusal to cooperate led to a lengthy investigation, and despite a series of setbacks an Information Tribunal

## SO, WHY DO WE HAVE TO PAY FOR THIS LOT? BLUE LABOUR

eventually backed the newspaper by declaring that the receipts should be released. The ruling prompted a futile High Court appeal, and by the end of 2008 it was decided that four years' worth of expenses – over a million receipts – should be published.

> People are sick of the cost of Parliament rising year after year
>
> **TAXPAYERS' ALLIANCE**

Once again, Parliament managed to delay the process. In January 2009, Leader of the Commons Harriet Harman tried unsuccessfully to have MPs' expenses excused from the FOIA, but while the data continued to be disputed a mole leaked expenses information to the *Daily Telegraph*.

The newspaper revealed in May 2009 that tourism minister Barbara Follett had claimed £25,000 for private security patrols around her London home, while some of her colleagues had "flipped" their second home addresses, enabling them to claim for repairs and furnishings on more than one property. Other luxuries paid for by an increasingly outraged public included tennis court repairs, moat maintenance and swimming pools, revelations that resulted in an instantaneous and highly damaging political scandal. Just days after the story broke, a record 3.8 million viewers tuned in to watch Labour MP Margaret Beckett being heckled on BBC1's *Question Time*.

Within days, MPs were queuing up to repay their expenses in a very public display of damage control – but the disclosures kept coming. Labour's Communities Secretary Hazel Blears was compelled to stump up £13,000 in dodged capitals gains tax, while former Labour MP Elliot

Morley was revealed to have claimed £16,000 for a mortgage he had already repaid in full. The former was one of many MPs forced to resign in disgrace over the scandal, while the latter confirmed he would not stand for re-election.

One of the more embarrassing claims was made by Home Secretary Jacqui Smith, who was exposed for claiming for films watched by her husband Richard Timney, two of which were pornographic. She later stated, "I was much more angry with [my husband] about the fact that we had not, between us, properly checked the expense claim than I was about the [nature of the] film. I think porn is wrong because of my feminist background, and I would argue with him about it, but it was as wrong for us to claim for [the non-pornographic films] *Surf's Up* and *Oceans 13* as it was for us to claim for porn."

As well as these high-profile cases, House of Commons Speaker Michael Martin was roundly criticized for overlooking the abuse of the expenses system, and for speaking out against MPs who defended the *Daily Telegraph*. He was also accused of focusing on *how* the information came to light as opposed to apologizing for the controversy, and subsequently resigned when it became clear that the Commons had lost faith in him.

Although a significant amount of money was paid back and an ongoing review of the expenses system promised, the scandal reappeared in September 2009 when the mole who leaked information to the *Daily Telegraph* explained that he had done so over his anger at the poor treatment of British troops in Afghanistan. According to the mole, some of them had resorted to moonlighting as guards for staff hired to sort through MPs' receipts, saying that

## THE GREAT MPs GRAVY TRAIN
# £93M
## ..and all at OUR expense
### FURY OVER HUGE BILL

the soldiers in question needed the extra work in order to pay for essential equipment. He explained: "It's not easy to watch footage on the news of a coffin draped in a Union Jack and then come in to work the next day and see on your computer what MPs are taking for themselves.

"The person looking at [Hazel Blears'] expenses was disgusted that she had claimed for a Kit Kat. Then Gordon Brown came up. It turned out we were paying for his Sky Sports package. No one could fathom why he was allowed to claim for that rather than watching BBC News 24 like other people."

# MPs MAKE US PAY £5M FOR THEIR CHEAP FOOD & DRINK

# WORDS OF WISDOM

"EVERYBODY SAYS IT, AND WHAT EVERYBODY SAYS MUST BE TRUE."

JAMES FENIMORE COOPER
(1789–1851)

# GENERATION SEX

"NEVER GET MARRIED IN THE MORNING, BECAUSE YOU NEVER KNOW WHO YOU'LL MEET THAT NIGHT."

PAUL HORNUNG, AMERICAN FOOTBALL PLAYER

# OSCAR WILDE

The incisive wit of Oscar Wilde made him one of the most eminent writers of the late Victorian era. His plays, short stories and one novel were liberally peppered with droll quotes such as the one below, and frequently explored the controversial theme of sexuality.

Despite flirting with social taboos, Wilde became a celebrity. Sadly, his achievements were soon overshadowed by a trial for gross indecency, a scandal that was far from tedious.

After breaking up with his first serious girlfriend, Oscar Wilde married Constance Lloyd in 1884. The couple had two children, but in 1891 Wilde embarked on an affair with Lord Alfred Douglas, a young man he affectionately referred to as Bosie. The true nature of Wilde's sexuality has been debated ever since.

By all accounts, Wilde and Constance enjoyed a happy union, but unsurprisingly the marriage failed to survive his interest in the clandestine gay world of the time, or his subsequent infatuation with Bosie. Constance eventually changed her surname to Holland and retreated to Switzerland with the children.

Bosie and Wilde's relationship was far from hidden, something that enraged Bosie's father, John Douglas, the 9th Marquis of Queensberry. Determined to separate the pair, he publicly accused Wilde of sodomy. Shaken by the slur, Wilde reacted by bringing a defamation suit against Queensberry, a move that backfired spectacularly. Shocking details of Wilde's private life were revealed, and the case received great attention from the press. Wilde was forced to back down before his reputation was damaged any further, but it was too late: shortly after the collapse of the libel trial, he was arrested for gross indecency.

Wilde was imprisoned at Holloway as he awaited trial. Beginning in April 1895, the trial saw Wilde giving a spirited defence of "the love that dare not speak its name". The jury failed to agree on a verdict and Wilde was granted bail. This freedom was short-lived, however, as his final trial resulted in conviction and the maximum possible sentence: two years' hard labour.

The result was a terrible blow for Wilde, who was moved between several prisons and suffered with poor health throughout his incarceration. To make his punishment even worse, he was initially forbidden from writing, but once this ban was lifted he immediately penned a lengthy letter to Bosie (this was eventually published under the title *De Profundis*).

Upon release and eager to avoid further ridicule, Wilde left England and travelled abroad. He settled in Paris, where he was struck with a fatal combination of meningitis and a severe ear infection. He passed away on 29th December 1900, aged 46.

# "SCANDAL IS GOSSIP MADE TEDIOUS BY MORALITY."

## OSCAR WILDE, LADY WINDERMERE'S FAN, 1892

# The Daily Mirror

### THE MORNING JOURNAL WITH THE SECOND LARGEST NET SALE.

No. 3,073.  |  Registered at the G.P.O. as a Newspaper.  |  FRIDAY, AUGUST 29, 1913  |  One Halfpenny.

## NOTABLE PRODUCTION OF "THE PICTURE OF DORIAN GRAY": TABLE ON WHICH OSCAR WILDE WROTE HIS NOVEL USED IN LAST NIGHT'S PLAY.

Last night London playgoers renewed their acquaintance with that young and versatile actor, M. Lou-Tellegen, who was leading man in the latest appearances here or Mme. Sarah Bernhardt. He is the new tenant of the Vaudeville Theatre, where he is presenting Miss Constant Lounsbery's dramatised version of Oscar Wilde's extraordinary novel, "The Picture of Dorian Gray." The table on which the late author wrote the script of his book is one of the properties. (1) Miss Julia James as Sybil Vane. (2, 3, 4 and 6) M. Lou-Tellegen in the title-role, and Miss James. (5) Dorian in a mad rage has killed his friend Basil Haliward (Mr. A. Scott Craven), the artist who painted the picture. (7) Dorian sees the change in the picture, but the change is the change in his own soul. He goes to stab the picture, but kills himself. M. Lou-Tellegen, it may be mentioned, mastered the English language in a fortnight.—(*Daily Mirror* photographs.)

CENTURY OF SCANDAL GENERATION SEX

"THERE IS ONLY ONE THING IN THE WORLD WORSE THAN BEING TALKED ABOUT, AND THAT IS NOT BEING TALKED ABOUT."

OSCAR WILDE, THE PICTURE OF DORIAN GRAY, 1891.

# HEADLINES FROM TIMES GONE BY

The enduring popularity of soap opera is a clear sign that audiences love a household drama – as long as it's not their own. With this in mind, it comes as little surprise that real-life soap operas have found their way into the headlines for as long as anyone can remember – just take a look at these vintage domestic disputes.

CENTURY OF SCANDAL GENERATION SEX

SATURDAY, APRIL 30, 1938

## Daily Mirror
No. 10733    Registered at the G.P.O. as a Newspaper    ONE PENNY

# DANCE MORALS TRIAL
## HELD UP BY ROARS OF VILLAGE

### Police Lose a King

### Three Judges Pass Sentence on Guilty Salome

### BOY DROWNED IN BATH GAME

### 'Her Head on His Shoulder'

### BRITAIN'S PLEDGE TO AID FRANCE

### THE QUEEN TO SEE "THE CUP"

How Love Began with you SEE PAGE 13

Hullo! Hullo! Hullo! It's a Different Girl Again!

---

## Daily Mirror
THE DAILY PICTURE    NEWSPAPER WITH THE LARGEST NET SALE

No. 10,050    registered at the G.P.O. as a Newspaper    SATURDAY, FEBRUARY 15, 1936    One Penny

Broadcasting - Pages 20 & 21

EUSTACE . . . . . Page 6
QUIET CORNER . . . 14
DOCTOR'S DIARY . . . 17
SERIAL . . . . . . 19
BELINDA . . . . . . 22

Amusements: Page 20

# RICH WOMAN WHO WED BUTLER
## Makes Him Happy with Seven Words

FROM OUR SPECIAL CORRESPONDENT

Mrs. Florence Collier

### Won't Share a Grave with Father-in-Law

### WIFE IN SHOTS TRAGEDY WAS LONDON 'PHONE GIRL

### Left Him After Quarrel

### Met in Paris

GOOD OMEN

### ARM SEVERED IN ROAD CRASH

### WARRANT ISSUED: FOUND DEAD

EX-PRINCE WORSE

---

# POISON TONGUE TORTURES RICH
## WIFE: SCANDAL BY TELEPHONE

---

# WRONGED WIFE STILL
## KEEPS BELIEF IN GUNMAN: "HE IS MY MAN"

# SIR JOHN GIELGUD

When Sir John Gielgud passed away in 2000, the 96-year-old actor had long been established as one of England's greatest performers and directors. He was the only Briton to have won an Emmy, a Grammy, an Oscar, and a Tony award, amassing countless other accolades during his eight decades in show business. Despite his veteran status, he also endured a "cottaging" scandal in 1953 that he feared would destroy his career. Homosexuality was still illegal at the time, and although his peers did not have an issue with his private life he dreaded public reaction to his conviction for "persistently importuning for immoral purposes

[in a London toilet]". Unsure of what would happen as a result of the indiscretion, Gielgud nevertheless honoured his work commitments and took to the stage shortly after, where he received a standing ovation from the audience. It appeared that the incident was less troublesome than he had anticipated, though Gielgud is said to have avoided Hollywood for a decade over concerns that his past would cause him to be ostracized.

**ABOVE:** Actor Sir John Gielgud (far right).

"WHEN THEY LOOK BACK ON ME I WANT 'EM TO REMEMBER ME NOT FOR ALL MY WIVES, ALTHOUGH I'VE HAD A FEW, AND CERTAINLY NOT FOR ANY MANSIONS OR HIGH LIVIN' MONEY I MADE AND SPENT. I WANT 'EM TO REMEMBER ME SIMPLY FOR MY MUSIC."

JERRY LEE LEWIS

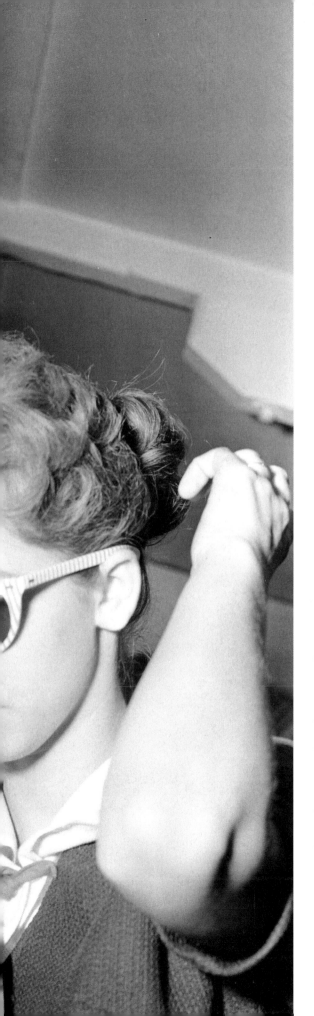

# JERRY LEE LEWIS

Pioneering rock 'n' roller Jerry Lee Lewis may be best known for his piano-led hits 'Great Balls of Fire' and 'Whole Lotta Shakin' Goin' On', but his dramatic live performances and controversial love life can't be forgotten either. Lewis' manic playing style involved standing on and kicking his keyboard, leading to a "wild man" tag that followed him into everyday life. In 1958, his third marriage caused huge controversy, not because 23-year-old Lewis had

married his cousin, but because she was only 13. His American career was destroyed by the scandal, and he disappeared from the spotlight almost immediately. It wasn't until the late 1960s that he was able to pull off a minor comeback, and even then he hadn't calmed his erratic behaviour completely; in the mid-1970s he accidentally shot his bass player Butch Owens during a live performance. Lewis later said that he thought the gun was unloaded, while Owens (who survived) said Lewis had been trying to shoot a bottle onstage. Lewis' career appears to have survived such setbacks, as he continues to tour the world today.

SLICED HUSBAND 'LIKED TO MAKE WOMEN SCREAM'

LORENA: 'Years of abuse'

BOBBITT: 'Showed true grit'

# JOHN AND LORENA BOBBIT

The shocking tale of John and Lorena Bobbit caused men the world over to cross their legs in disbelief and horror.

On 23rd June 1993, John returned home from a night of heavy drinking and allegedly assaulted his wife. After he passed out, Lorena proceeded to the kitchen and grabbed a large knife, which she used to sever off more than half of her husband's penis. She then drove away,

throwing the grim trophy into a field before calling the police and confessing. Luckily for John, the severed organ was recovered and successfully reattached.

When the case went to court, Lorena explained that she was a long-suffering victim of domestic abuse and had finally "snapped" on the night of the incident. Several witnesses corroborated her claims, while her husband's unreliable testimony also added weight to the accusations. She was found not guilty after the court ruled that temporary insanity had caused the impulse to sexually wound her husband.

The couple divorced in 1995, with John going on to achieve minor fame after appearing in two adult films, *John Wayne Bobbitt: Uncut* and *Frankenpenis*.

# Wife cried rape months before her knife attack

# PARIS HILTON

In early 2003, Paris Hilton was primarily known for being a New York socialite and heir to the Hilton hotel fortune. She had already achieved moderate success as a model, and her enviable combination of good looks and staggering wealth ensured she was invited to every party in town.

That year, her burgeoning media profile went up a notch when she met the comedy department at FOX. They were pitching a show in which two well-heeled youngsters would move in with a working-class family, carry out menial chores and generally learn about the lives of "ordinary" people. Paris and her childhood friend Nicole Richie were perfect for the job.

The show was named *The Simple Life* and was little more than an excuse to watch Paris and Nicole as they failed to perform even the most basic of everyday tasks. The programme was in the can by December 2003, but was almost entirely derailed one week before its premiere by an unexpected scandal: Paris Hilton's sex tape.

## Paris's nightmare

Curriculum Vitae

**Paris Hilton**

**DOB:** 17/02/1981

**Work experience:**
Singer, reality television star, perfumiere, actress, handbag designer, author

**Hobbies and interests:**
Collects small dogs, home videos, drinking, driving (not together, of course), presidential campaigner

# PARIS IS FEELING TOUCHY

## Hilton pants for attention at club

# PARIS IN THE FLINGTIME

Just as *The Simple Life* was about to air, numerous gossip websites posted a homemade tape depicting Hilton performing a sex act on ex-boyfriend Rick Salomon, who also acted as cameraman. The grainy footage, reportedly taken in 2001, was filmed entirely in night vision, giving its stars an alien look of green skin and jet black eyes. Details surrounding the leak remain sketchy, but once online it spread like wildfire.

Although *The Simple Life* opened to huge viewing figures, Salomon and the Hiltons were far from happy. The former launched a $10 million defamation suit against Paris' family after they intimated that she was inebriated in the footage; meanwhile, the Hiltons sued Panama-based Internet company Kahatani Ltd for $30 million, claiming it had illegally distributed the tape and violated Paris' privacy in the process. In a surprise turn of events, Salomon acquired the rights to the footage while the Hilton's case was thrown out of court.

Salomon wasted no time in capitalizing on this new-found ownership, releasing the tape as a heavily marketed DVD entitled *1 Night in Paris*. Hilton tried to block the release and eventually settled out of court, with some reports indicating that she received a $400,000 payout and a cut of future royalties from each DVD sale.

Amazingly, Hilton's career went from strength to strength after the sex tape debacle. She is now an established businesswoman, earning millions from her reality TV work, public appearances, fragrances, books, movie roles, fashion lines and even her own pop album. Some may wonder why she continues to work, but it's a good thing she does – in 2007, her grandfather Barron Hilton reportedly diverted most of his estate into a charitable foundation after becoming exasperated by the bad behaviour of his grandchildren.

# SEX-ON-BEACH BRIT SAYS: I WILL GO BACK TO DUBAI

CENTURY OF SCANDAL GENERATION SEX

BY **VICTORIA WARD**
victoria.ward@mirror.co.uk

**A BRITISH businessman jailed for having sex on a Dubai beach wants to return to the Arab state.**

Vince Acors, 34, who was deported after being given three months for outraging public decency with fellow Brit Michelle Palmer, said he still hoped to trade there.

Although he is banned from the United Arab Emirates for three years, the telecoms firm boss yesterday said he would appeal to be allowed to return. He added: "Hopefully over the next few months I will see significant inroads into Dubai."

His sentence was suspended on appeal and he arrived back in the UK on Christmas Eve. He denied he and Palmer had sex but admitted "physical contact" on Jumeirah Beach on July 5.

Acors, from Bromley, Kent, met Palmer, of Oakham, Rutland, at a champagne brunch where "your glass is never empty". He admitted they made poor decisions and said he had "horrific" experiences during 10 days in jail.

The dad of one added: "I can't see myself and Michelle pursuing a relationship."

▶ **HOPE** Acors yesterday and, right, Palmer

88

# SEX ON BEACH BRITS JAILED FOR 3 MONTHS

## Couple stunned by Dubai verdict

## SEX ON THE BEACH

Two over-amorous Brits were threatened with jail when they were caught apparently having sex on a Dubai beach, though they insisted they had only been "kissing and cuddling".

The embarrassing scandal dominated the headlines in summer 2008, especially when the couple, Michelle Palmer, 36, and Vince Acors, 34, were revealed to have been drunk at the time.

Both were fined and sentenced to three months in jail for the crimes of unmarried sex and public indecency, though an appeal saw the pair being deported without serving any prison time. Speaking after the second verdict, Palmer said: "It just proves our innocence after all the bad stuff that was written."

**WILL PAYNE**
will.payne@mirror.co.uk

**A BRITISH couple caught having sex on a beach were both jailed for three months yesterday.**

Police spotted Vince Acors and Michelle Palmer on Dubai's Jumeirah sands in the early hours.

They were asked to move on at first but were arrested when caught in the act a second time, officers said.

Acors, 34, and Palmer, 36, were found guilty of having unmarried sex and public indecency, both breaches of the Muslim state's strict laws.

They also admitted being drunk in public and were fined £160. The couple, still out on bail in Dubai, have 15 days to appeal.

Divorced dad Acors, of Bromley, Kent, and Palmer, of Oakham, Rutland, were both devastated.

One colleague of Palmer, sacked from her job as a publishing boss in Dubai, said: "She is depressed and has panic attacks. She just wants to go home to her family."

Palmer met holidaymaker Acors, boss of an SMS text company, only on the day of their arrest – at a £60 all-you-can-drink champagne brunch.

It is thought she was a regular on the expat party scene.

The couple have always claimed they were just "kissing and hugging" rather than having sex.

Their lawyer Hassam Matter confirmed he would appeal.

He said: "They are not guilty but they were prepared for this. I told them before that I thought the judge would give this verdict."

But prosecutor Faisal Abdelmalek said he was disappointed with what he called the "light" sentence.

Pauline Crowe, who heads the UK charity Prisoners Abroad, said the case should serve as a warning.

She added: "It is crucial that Britons are fully aware of local laws and customs and that they respect and adhere to these."

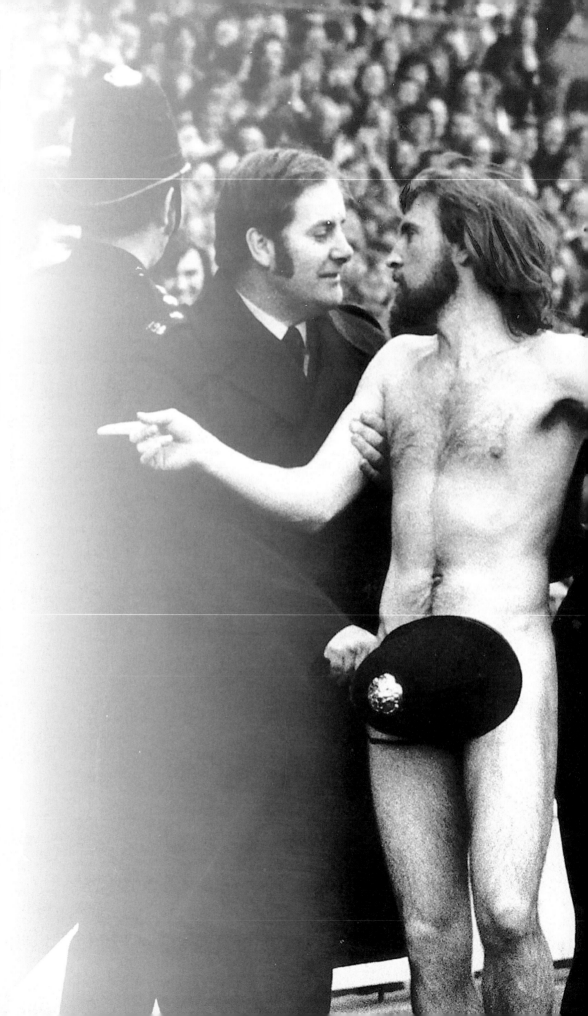

WORDS OF WISDOM

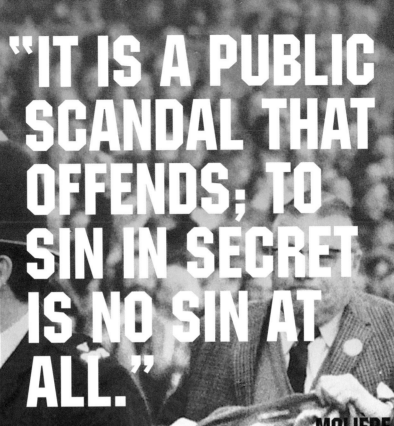

# "IT IS A PUBLIC SCANDAL THAT OFFENDS; TO SIN IN SECRET IS NO SIN AT ALL."

**MOLIÈRE**

91

# BREEDING IS NO BARRIER

"LIKE ALL THE BEST FAMILIES, WE HAVE OUR SHARE OF ECCENTRICITIES, OF IMPETUOUS AND WAYWARD YOUNGSTERS AND OF FAMILY DISAGREEMENTS."

QUEEN ELIZABETH II

"I HAVE FOUND IT IMPOSSIBLE TO CARRY THE HEAVY BURDEN OF RESPONSIBILITY AND TO DISCHARGE MY DUTIES AS KING AS I WOULD WISH TO DO WITHOUT THE HELP AND SUPPORT OF THE WOMAN I LOVE."

KING EDWARD VIII

# KING EDWARD VIII AND MRS WALLIS SIMPSON

When Edward met American socialite Wallis Simpson in 1931, she was already in her second marriage. He, on the other hand, was the most eligible bachelor around and courting the latest in a long line of mistresses. In certain circles he was becoming known as the playboy prince, something his father, King George V, was none too happy about.

George feared Edward's irresponsibility and would have preferred the prince's younger brother, Albert, to succeed to the throne since he was already happily married with children, the Princesses Elizabeth and Margaret. Edward, on the other hand, was determined to play the field for as long as possible. This all changed, however, when Edward met Wallis at a party.

Their inauspicious introduction eventually turned into an affair, and the unlikely pair would meet when Wallis' husband Ernest was travelling. The relationship was consummated by 1934, and Wallis' marriage was beginning to suffer. Despite reports that Wallis was becoming exasperated by Edward's increasingly lapdog-like behaviour, they were still an item when King George passed away in January 1936. Later that year, Wallis was granted a decree nisi from her second husband, meaning she would soon be able to remarry.

King George died before his reservation

about his son was realized. Edward ascended the throne as King Edward VIII immediately after his father's death, and by the end of the year his relationship with Wallis had come into the open. Public outrage caused her to flee to France, but Edward had no intention of separating from Wallis. In fact, he wanted to marry her.

The idea that a new king would make his twice-married American mistress Queen of England was unthinkable, and a suggestion from Edward that she receive a lesser title was also quashed. Realizing that the public were unlikely to accept Wallis in any role, Edward chose to abdicate after less than a year. As he handed over the role of king to Prince Albert (who was crowned as King George VI), Edward told the nation: "I have found it impossible to carry the heavy burden of responsibility and to discharge my duties as King as I would wish to do without the help and support of the woman I love."

Edward waited for Wallis' decree absolute to be granted before reuniting with her in Austria in mid-1937. They married in France that year, to become the Duke and Duchess of Windsor – but the new titles they had been afforded were not enough to persuade any of Edward's family to attend.

Unfortunately, the newlyweds could not seem to stay away from controversy. In 1937 they made an ill-advised trip to Germany as personal guests of Adolf Hitler. After this they settled in France until the outbreak of war in 1939, at which point they moved around Europe, continuing to worry the British government by appearing to sympathize with the Nazis. Eventually they were moved to the Bahamas in an attempt to keep them out of trouble, only returning to France once the war had ended.

They became popular figures in their adoptive country, and Edward made occasional contact with his family. Despite this, Wallis was never truly accepted and only stayed at Buckingham Palace when she came to London for Edward's funeral in 1972. She died in Paris in 1986 and was buried at Windsor alongside her husband.

# Daily Mirror

FRI
SEPT 23
1955

2ᵈ

FORWARD
WITH THE PEOPLE

No. 16,107

# AMAZIN
# OF TH
# WHO WANTED

## THE KING WHO WANTED A SON

In 1955, the *Daily Mirror* reported on a most unusual state of affairs within Libya's monarchy: 65-year-old King Idris had failed to sire a son. Fearing his reign could be terminated by a ruthless family member (next in line was his brother, and after that the first male cousin), Idris persuaded his wife Fatima that he needed a second bride with whom to try to produce a male heir. Amazingly, two sons then arrived when both wives fell pregnant at the same time. Unluckily for everybody concerned, however, Idris was deposed in a bloodless coup 14 years later, so neither of the sons made it to the throne.

## Now both his wives are to have babies

**Daily Mirror Correspondent, Cairo, Thursday**

A KING who married a second wife three months ago, in the hope of having a son to succeed to his throne, will soon have children by BOTH his queens.

Both may present him with a son, in which case the first to be born will be heir to the throne.

### He Is Sixty-Five

This amazing situation has arisen at the court of King Idris of Libya.

The King, who is sixty-five, was married to Wife No. 1, Queen Fatima, twenty years ago.

A son born to them died in infancy.

The years went by . . . no other son was born . . . the King's brother, Emir Mohammed Rida Mahdi Senussi, became Heir-Apparent.

### Intrigue

Then Fatima agreed that while her husband had no son he was in danger.

At any time, she knew, there could be an attempt to grab the throne by intriguing cousins and relatives.

Fatima herself approved the King's choice of Miss Aliya Abdel Lamloun, daugh-

98

# STORY KING A SON

WIFE No. 1      WIFE No. 2

## THE KING WHO WAITS

ter of a wealthy Egyptian Bedouin chieftain, as Wife No. 2.

The Moslem wedding took place on June 5.

Queen Aliya was installed in the Royal Palace.

Now, within days of each other, Queen Fatima, 50, and Queen Aliya, 38, have told the King that they are to be mothers.

### Doctors Called

Doctors were called in They confirmed the news and said that both babies were due about six months from now.

But no doctor was certain enough to prophesy which baby would be born first and—if it is a boy — become Libya's future king.

Palace officials are holding their breath. In the royal quarters both queens offer up their fervent prayers to Allah.

### Faithful Queen

In the bazaars of Libya the hope is that a son will be born first to Fatima, the faithful queen for twenty-years.

For Allah, they argue solemnly, is merciful.

And if after all these years he has had pity on Fatima, is he going to withdraw his mercy on her by letting Queen Aliya, the new wife provide the heir to the throne?

*Advertiser's Announcement*

Milk Chocolate tumbling over creamy caramel — dreamy centre!

PUNCH MY'S MILK FUDGE

the Big Top in treats!

ONLY 4ᴰ

ABOVE: Princess
Margaret and
Lord Snowdon.

# PRINCESS MARGARET

Before Diana and Fergie became tabloid fodder, there was Princess Margaret. Queen Elizabeth II's younger sister first caused unease within the monarchy in 1953, when she announced her desire to marry divorcee Peter Townsend. Townsend was 16 years her senior and had been a great friend to her late father, King George VI. Elizabeth informed her sister she would lose her right to succession if she went ahead with the wedding, and a distraught Margaret opted to call the whole thing off.

Margaret found a new partner in the shape of photographer Antony Armstrong-Jones, and the couple's 1960 wedding was the first of its kind to be televised. Two children followed – Viscount Linley and Lady Sarah – and Margaret and Antony were re-titled as Countess and Earl of Snowdon.

Although the Snowdons regularly socialized in glamorous circles and seemed to epitomize

# Daily Mirror

SAT FEB. 27 1960

2½ + No. 17,480

# PRINCESS MARGARET ENGAGED

Antony Armstrong-Jones
*He is a photographer, aged 29.*

**P**RINCESS MARGARET is to marry a commoner —Antony Armstrong-Jones, the Society photographer.

The announcement that surprised the world came from Clarence House last night while Mr. Armstrong-Jones, 29— the same age as Margaret—was week-ending at Royal Lodge, Windsor, with the Queen Mother and the Princess.

A Buckingham Palace spokesman said later that the Queen and Prince Philip said they were "delighted, because this is such an obviously happy match."

The Queen has asked Mr. Armstrong-Jones to stay at Buckingham Palace so that he can be in close touch with all the people making arrangements for the wedding.

The date has not yet been fixed and no plans have been made for the couple's future home.

## Billy Wallace in the Secret

Mr. Billy Wallace, one of Princess Margaret's closest friends, said at his Mayfair home last night: "This is splendid. I have never known two people better suited to each other.

"They have been unofficially engaged for quite a long time.

"I think it is terribly satisfactory that Princess Margaret and a few of her friends have managed to keep the secret."

Four years ago, on November 30, 1955, Princess Margaret dramatically renounced the love of Group-Captain Peter Townsend, now 45. He wed twenty-year-old Marie-Luce Jamagne, daughter of a wealthy Belgian company director, last December.

She said last night: " Peter and I have known about the engagement for some time."

101

the swinging Sixties, rumours began to fly that all was not well behind the scenes. By 1973, Margaret had been introduced to a young man named Roddy Llewellyn, and the pair regularly holidayed together in Mustique despite a 17-year age gap – not to mention her marriage. There was even speculation that Margaret once overdosed after a dramatic falling-out with Llewellyn.

Photographs of Margaret and her toy-boy

# FEARS FOR MARGARET

**ABOVE AND RIGHT:** Princess Margaret's wedding.

inevitably found their way into the tabloids, and the Snowdons were forced to announce their separation. The press and public turned on Margaret, even though Antony remarried just months after their divorce. By this point Margaret's relationship with Llewellyn was all but over, though the two remained friends.

Sadly, Margaret suffered with ill-health in her later years and died in 2002 after a series of strokes.

STARTS TODAY !

A NEW REVEALING LOOK AT THE ROYALS

# The Greatest Show on Earth

"HELP ME, HE'S IN THE HOUSE, HE'S MURDERED THE NANNY."

LADY LUCAN

# LORD LUCAN

On the evening of 7th November 1974, British aristocrat Richard John Bingham, seventh Earl of Lucan, fled the scene of a grisly murder at his ex-wife Lady Lucan's house. He then made a number of calls and visits to various acquaintances before vanishing completely in the early hours of the following morning. His disappearance remains unsolved to this day.

Lady Lucan told police he had attacked and killed their children's nanny, Sandra Rivett, before launching an attack on her. When she managed to escape and raise the alarm she ran straight to a nearby pub, the Plumber's Arms, telling anyone who would listen, "Help me, he's in the house, he's murdered the nanny." She later confirmed to police that "he" was her ex-husband.

When police arrived at the house that evening, the three Lucan children were thankfully found unharmed. Further investigation of the large Belgravia property revealed a basement room covered in blood and male footprints, as well as the body of Rivett inside a sack. She had been beaten to death with a blunt instrument, and a bloodied piece of lead piping was found nearby. The back door leading to the room was unlocked, and the basement light bulb had been removed.

While this was going on, Lucan made two phone calls. The first was to his friend Madeleine Florman, who said afterwards that she recognized Lucan's voice and that he sounded distressed and incoherent. Shortly before the call she had been awoken by her doorbell, which she had ignored, thinking it was local youths playing a trick. Blood spots were

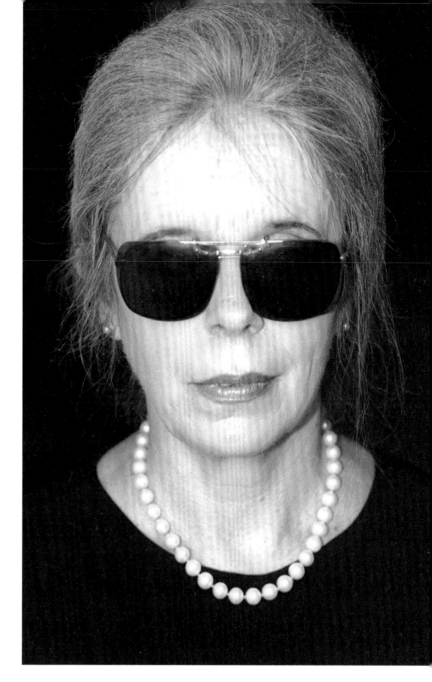

later found on her doorstep.

Lucan also made another call, this time to his mother. He informed her that he had witnessed a distressing altercation in the basement of his ex-wife's house but had been unable to intervene. He then asked his mother to go to the house and collect the three children, which she duly did.

Lucan then drove 40 miles to the Sussex home of his friends Ian and Susan Maxwell-Scott. He found Susan alone and recounted an embellished version of the story he had told his mother. According to Maxwell-Scott, Lucan

**ABOVE:**
Lady Lucan.

105

accusing Lucan of murder.

After speaking to Maxwell-Scott and using her telephone to check with his mother that she had collected the children, Lucan attempted to call his brother-in-law, Bill Shand-Kydd. When Shand-Kydd failed to answer, Lucan wrote him two letters and asked Maxwell-Scott to post them. He then left his friends' house and disappeared for ever. The car he had driven that night was later found abandoned, containing bloodstains and a piece of lead piping similar to that found at the crime scene.

An inquest the following year named Lord Lucan as the murderer of Sandra Rivett, though it was assumed he had intended to kill his wife only. As there was no light in the basement, claimed to have seen an intruder attacking his ex-wife, but upon entering the basement he had slipped on a pool of blood and given the assailant a chance to flee. Lady Lucan apparently then accused her ex-husband of hiring the man to kill her, hence running to the Plumber's Arms and

---

# Daily Mirror

EUROPE'S BIGGEST DAILY SALE

5p Tuesday, November 12, 1974 No. 22,024

## Dragnet for the murder-riddle Earl

# WHERE DID HE GO?

### Sacked! Exit for actress Mary

From MARK DOWDNEY in New York

ACTRESS Mary Ure hit out angrily last night after being fired on the eve of the Broadway opening of her latest play.

"I have no idea why I was replaced," she said. "I'm not sick, I'm not drunk and I'm not late."

The dramatic dismissal of one of Britain's best-known actresses came immediately after a preview matinee perform...

**OUT: Mary Ure.**

ance of the play "Love For Love" on Saturday.

Director Hal Prince ordered Mary's understudy, 25-year-old American Glenn Close, to take over for the show that evening.

Glenn, who finished drama school only last year, kept the leading lady role at the play's official opening last night.

Mary, the 41-year-old wife of actor-playwright Robert Shaw, said:

"It's a mystery why I have been fired. I got rave reviews from Boston's toughest critic."

**IN: Glenn Close.**

after the two-week try-out in Philadelphia.

Hal Prince, one of Broadway's most successful directors, would only say last night: "Miss Ure has been replaced."

But he is reported to have said that she "didn't communicate with the audience."

Mary has been in America rehearsing the William Congreve play since early September.

**SURPRISED: Mrs. Maxwell Scott. Picture: GEOFFREY DAY**

## VISIT AT MIDNIGHT

By PHILIP MELLOR

A FRIEND of Lord Lucan spoke yesterday of her late-night meeting with the earl in her Victorian country mansion.

Mrs. Susan Maxwell Scott told how Lord Lucan turned up at her home in Uckfield, Sussex, only hours after the murder of the nanny in London.

Mrs. Maxwell Scott said: "My husband was

in London and I was alone apart from two of my six children who were asleep upstairs.

"I was surprised when Lord Lucan arrived at that late hour.

"I invited him in and we sat and chatted over a cup of coffee in the sitting-room for a couple of hours.

"I offered him a meal, but he did not want one.

"We had a long talk, then he sat down and wrote two letters.

"He gave me the two letters and I posted them for him."

The letters were both addressed to a relative by marriage, Mr. William Shand-Kydd, a prominent amateur jockey, at his home in Cambridge Square, Bayswater, London.

In one letter, the earl

● Continued on Page Two

### Guard

Meanwhile, an armed guard was put on his injured wife in a London hospital.

A policeman and a policewoman, each carrying a gun, stayed near her bed at St. George's, Hyde Park Corner.

Police are holding Lord Lucan's passport, but he

By TOM TULLETT
Chief of the Mirror Crime Bureau

SCOTLAND YARD murder squad detectives were baffled last night by the disappearance of Lord Lucan.

He is being sought for questioning about the murder of his children's nanny and a vicious attack on his wife.

A dragnet put out by police in Britain and France failed to produce any lead to the 39-year-old Earl's whereabouts.

could use a temporary one to leave the country.

Throughout yesterday detectives followed up dozens of reports that the Earl had been sighted.

Police are satisfied that they know the killer's identity.

The Countess has given detectives an account of what happened in her house in Belgravia, but Detective Chief Superintendent Roy Ranson, who is leading the hunt, said: "I cannot comment on what she told us."

### Screams

He revealed that several people were being interviewed.

Lady Lucan, who has serious head injuries, has told detectives that she spoke to the killer.

Police believe the Countess was attacked and fled after screams brought nanny Sandra Rivett to her aid.

Mrs. Rivett was killed outright with a piece of lead piping.

Lord Lucan was heard after the killer fled and staggered to a public house for help.

LORD LUCAN: His passport held.

# I'VE CAUGHT LORD LUCAN

investigators concluded that Lucan had simply got the wrong woman. He and Lady Lucan had been through a bitter divorce and custody battle, and this was given as his motive.

Lord Lucan's disappearance led to a wave of sightings around the globe, though Lady Lucan and friends of Lucan have publicly stated their belief that he committed suicide.

Although the absent Lord was declared legally dead in 1999, "finding Lucan" remains a popular activity. In 2003, former Scotland Yard detective Duncan MacLaughlin published a book entitled *Dead Lucky: Lord Lucan, The Final Truth*, in which he claimed that Lucan had started a new life in Goa, India. According to

MacLaughlin's book, Lucan was now known as Barry Halpin, and pictures of Halpin taken in 1991 did seem to bear a resemblance to Lucan. However, MacLaughlin's claims were dismissed when a friend of Halpin's identified him as having lived in Liverpool in the 1960s. Another "sighting" in 2007 claimed that Lucan was living in a van in New Zealand, but this was also queried after the alleged "Lucan" stated he was a different height… and 10 years younger than the real Lucan.

If Lord Lucan is still alive, he will turn 76 in December 2010.

# I SAW LORD LUCAN

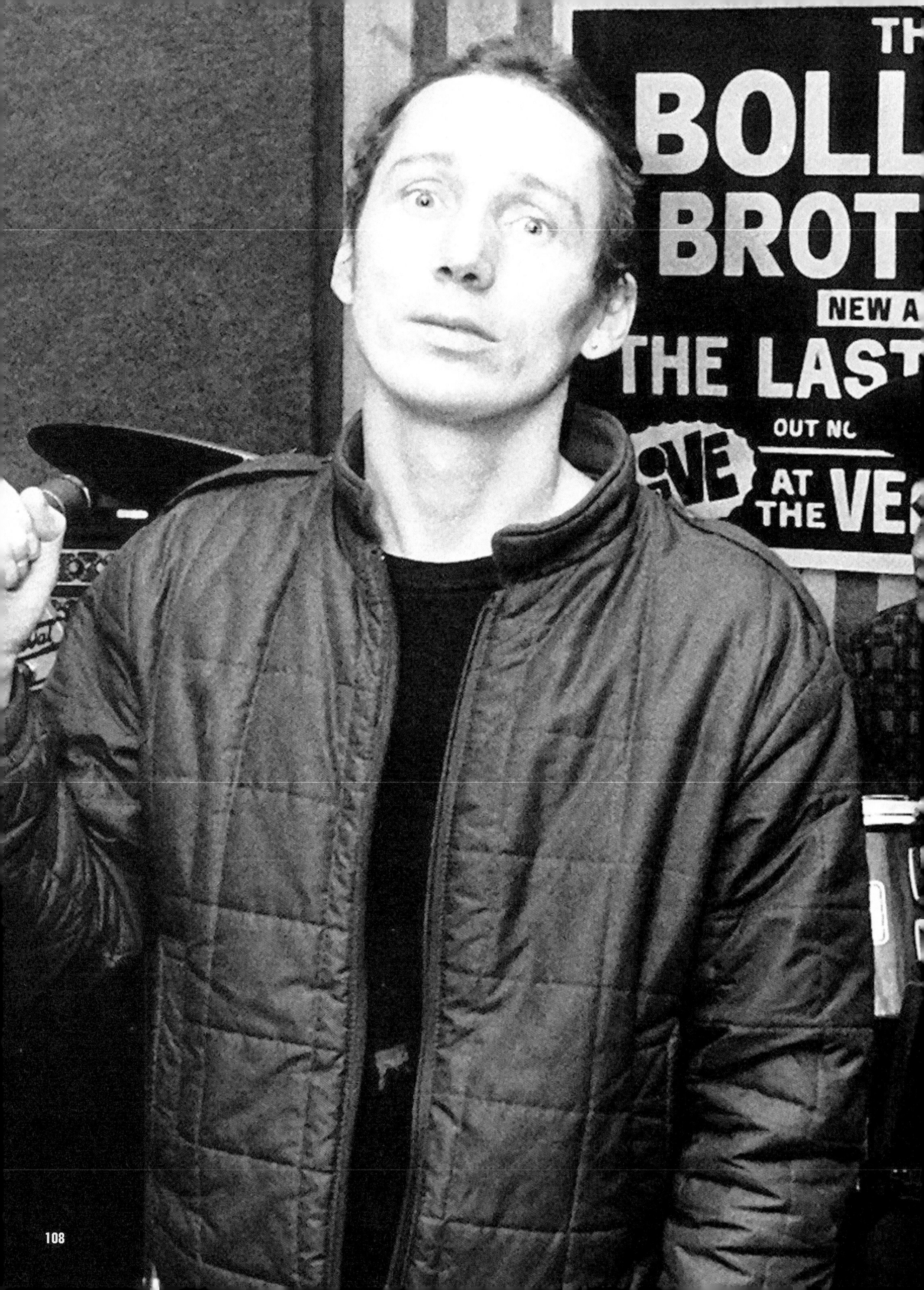
TH
BOLL
BROT
NEW A
THE LAST
OUT NC
AT
THE VE

# AN INTRUDER IN BUCKINGHAM PALACE

Queen Elizabeth II was most surprised to find an intruder in her bedroom on 9th July 1982.

Not only had 32-year-old Michael Fagan evaded Buckingham Palace's armed police, soldiers and security guards, he had also made it past maids, surveillance cameras and numerous electronic bugging devices intended to keep Her Majesty safe. In an even more staggering turn of events, it was later revealed that this was his second unauthorized visit. Fagan's first foray into the palace had not led him to the Queen, though after scaling a palace drainpipe and entering through a roof window he decided to take a memento, grabbing half a bottle of wine as he left.

His second entry was more eventful. After cutting his hand on an ashtray, a bleeding Fagan made his way to the Queen's bedroom. She was disturbed by a twitching curtain and soon realized somebody else was in the room, but instead of panicking the 56-year-old monarch calmly sat and chatted to Fagan for 10 minutes. As the pair discussed the joys of parenthood – both had four children – the Queen was able to make two phone calls to the palace switchboard. The gravity of the situation was not picked up on by palace officials, however, and it was only when a maid chanced upon the unfolding drama that Fagan was finally removed.

Fagan was not charged with trespassing since a criminal trial would have compromised the Queen's role as Head of State; he was instead charged with the theft of half a bottle of wine. The charge was dropped after Fagan underwent psychiatric evaluation, which saw him being sent to a secure mental health facility for three months. Fagan's mother later stated: "He thinks so much of the Queen. I can imagine him just wanting to simply talk and say hello and discuss his problems."

FAGAN: He said a little voice in his head sent him to the Palace

## FAGAN
### YES He did break into the Palace
### YES He did drink Charles's wine
### YES He did sit on the Queen's bed
### BUT THE VERDICT WAS:
# NOT GUILTY!

MICHAEL FAGAN, the man who sat on the Queen's bed, freely admitted an astonishing series of royal adventures yesterday.

He said that he had twice climbed into Buckingham Palace—and he claimed he was doing the Queen a favour. "Her security was no good and I proved it," he said.

Fagan told how he had drunk wine which was sent to Prince Charles to wet the royal baby's head. "I was thirsty, I had done a hard day's work for the Queen." And he claimed he had even sat on the throne.

But the verdict of an Old Bailey jury on Fagan was: Not guilty.

Fagan, 32, had been charged yesterday only with stealing half-a-bottle of wine. The jury was told they had to be satisfied he intended dishonestly to deprive the owner of the wine.

After a 14-minute adjournment, the jury of seven men and five women returned and announced their verdict.

There were gasps in court — and then a moment of absolute silence. Fagan looked delighted.

Afterwards, his father said: "The family are overjoyed, but it was a predictable result."

● Mirror Comment—See Page 2
● Gasp of Surprise—Pages 2 and 3
● The Queen's story—Centre Pages

DAILY Mirror

Friday, September 24, 1982        16p        ★ ★ ★

"THERE WERE THREE OF US
IN THIS MARRIAGE, SO IT
WAS A BIT CROWDED."

DIANA, PRINCESS OF WALES

# DIANA, PRINCESS OF WALES

When Prince Charles and Lady Diana wed in 1981, a global audience of 750 million tuned in to watch. People were thrilled when the potential future king and queen produced two sons, Princes William and Harry, and understandably disappointed when the golden couple announced their separation in 1992. The split proved to be less than amicable, with both parties admitting to infidelity in sensational television interviews.

Rumours of discord between Diana and Charles had been circulating for some time, and once the break-up became official Charles resumed his pre-Diana relationship with Camilla Parker Bowles. It later transpired that they had privately been seeing one another while Charles was still married, something Diana confirmed in her 1995 interview with the BBC's *Panorama* programme. The revelation "there were three of us in this marriage, so it was a bit crowded" became one of her most famous statements, and Diana also admitted to consequently conducting her own affair with riding instructor James Hewitt.

Such declarations were highly damaging to the Royal Family, and in late 1995 the Queen urged the "warring Waleses" to finalize their divorce as soon as possible. The marriage was officially over within a year, and Diana's title changed from Her Royal Highness to Diana, Princess of Wales. She became involved with

# I LOVED JAMES HEWITT

**AFFAIR: James Hewitt**

## HER AMAZING STORY: 16-PAGE SPECIAL

high-profile and occasionally controversial charity work, most memorably when she angered government ministers by visiting a landmine-strewn area of Angola.

In 1997, Diana became linked with Dodi Al-Fayed, the son of Harrods' owner and Egyptian billionaire Mohammed Al-Fayed. That summer, she and her sons were photographed holidaying with Dodi on his multi-million pound yacht, and

the press speculated that the two were very much an item. Tragically, their brief summer romance was to end in a horrifying accident that plunged the world into grief.

On 31st August 1997, Diana and Dodi were killed when their car crashed into a pillar in Paris' Pont de l'Alma tunnel. They and their bodyguard, Trevor Rees-Jones, had been involved in a high-speed pursuit with a number of paparazzi cars, and their driver, Henri Paul, had been drinking. Rees-Jones was the only survivor, and Paul was posthumously held partially responsible for the collision.

News of Diana's death resulted in an unprecedented outpouring of grief around the world. An enraged Mohammed Al-Fayed immediately claimed that a conspiracy was to blame, telling the press, "This is not an accident. It is a plot, an assassination." In 2008 he presented a multi-point conspiracy theory to a coroner, his main allegation being that Prince

# ROYAL WORLD EXCLUSIVE

# DI'S NEW MAN IS AL FAYED'S SON

LOVEBOAT: Di and Dodi on her holiday with the Al Fayeds

**By JAMES WHITAKER**
Royal Correspondent

PRINCESS Diana has found love again – with the playboy son of Harrods boss Mohamed Al Fayed.

Diana, 36, returned to Britain yesterday after a secret holiday with Dodi, 41, on his father's yacht in Corsica.

The princess shared a family break with the Al Fayeds in St Tropez last month. Then last Thursday, Diana and Dodi flew out on his father's private jet for their idyllic six days at sea. He is a millionaire film-maker who has dated a string of beauties.

A source said last night: "It could be true love, they are both lovely people."

Dodi said simply: "We are very good friends." His father, whose cash for questions accusations helped topple the Tories, is said to be glowing with pride.

Philip, Duke of Edinburgh, had used MI6 to orchestrate the "murder". The case collapsed as an inquest ruled that the three victims were unlawfully killed due to the "gross negligence" of driver Henri Paul and the paparazzi. Al-Fayed strongly disagreed with the outcome, despite the fact that Princes William and Harry said they "agreed" with the findings. He eventually dropped his decade-long fight, finally ending the scandal for good by saying: "Enough is enough, and for the sake of the two princes… I am not doing anything anymore."

**ABOVE:**
Mohammed
Al-Fayed.

114

# WORDS OF WISDOM

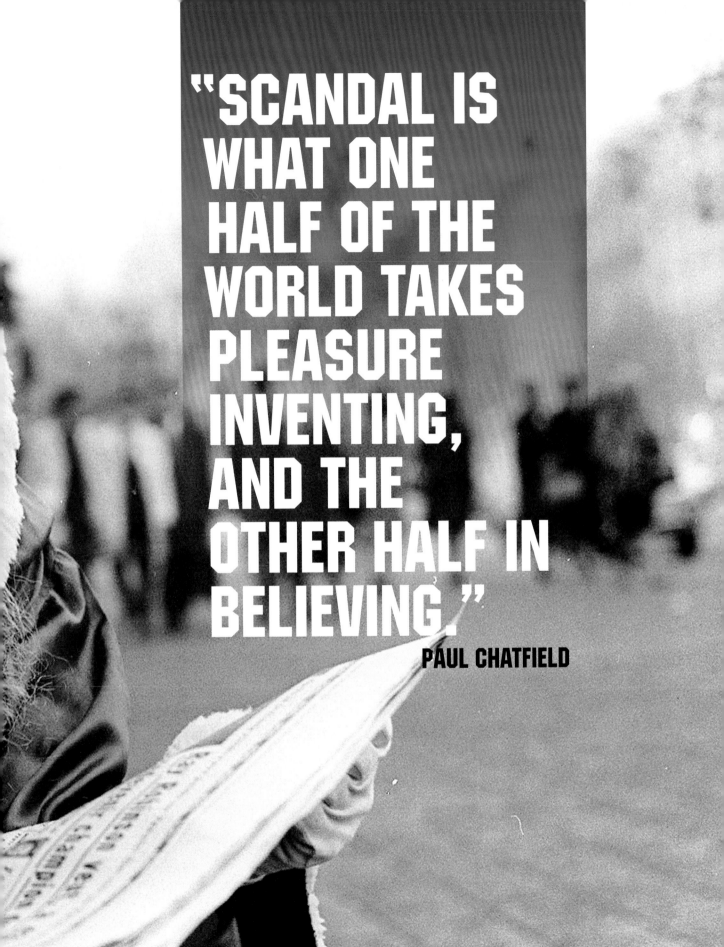

"SCANDAL IS WHAT ONE HALF OF THE WORLD TAKES PLEASURE INVENTING, AND THE OTHER HALF IN BELIEVING."

**PAUL CHATFIELD**

# SILVER
# SCREEN

"HOLLYWOOD IS A PLACE
WHERE A MAN CAN GET
STABBED IN THE BACK
WHILE CLIMBING A LADDER."

**WILLIAM FAULKNER (1897–1962)**

# FATTY ARBUCKLE

Roscoe "Fatty" Arbuckle was a giant of silent film in more ways than one. The larger-than-life actor was a major celebrity of the 1910s, reportedly earning up to $3 million a year by 1918 – a staggering amount for the time. He was a pioneering and influential comedian, and audiences loved the unlikely spectacle of his giant frame dealing effortlessly and gracefully with the physical demands of slapstick comedy. Unfortunately for Arbuckle, his industry and adoring public were quick to turn on him when he was arrested and tried for the gruesome death of 26-year-old Virginia Rappe, a young actress who passed away just days after falling ill at one of his parties.

The gathering took place in 1921, two years after prohibition had been introduced. The booze ban did not prevent Arbuckle and his friends from acquiring significant quantities of alcohol for their party, which would reflect badly on Arbuckle when details of the event were later revealed in court.

The men hired a suite in a San Francisco hotel and were joined by a number of female guests, including Rappe. At a certain point in the festivities

SECOND TRIAL.—Roscoe Arbuckle, whose second trial on a charge of the manslaughter of Miss Virginia Rappe, a cinema actress, ended yesterday without result. The jury disagreed and were dismissed.

FUNERAL OF V
Rappe, the film s
placed in

Crushed to death by a cruel clown

she fell seriously ill in Arbuckle's room, and a hotel doctor was summoned to examine her. He incorrectly surmised that she was intoxicated and prescribed medicine to calm her down, though she was eventually admitted to hospital with severe internal injuries.

At the hospital, a friend claimed that Arbuckle had raped Rappe, though doctors found no evidence to support her claims. Shortly afterwards, Rappe passed away as a result of complications from a ruptured bladder, and her friend then reported Arbuckle to the police – this time claiming that his large frame had caused Rappe's injuries. Rappe's lawyer went even further, telling the press that Arbuckle had sexually assaulted his former client with a large object. Many newspapers later reported that a champagne bottle had been used to violate her, though this was never proven.

The story took on a life of its own. Rappe's horrific death and Arbuckle's fame proved an irresistible combination for the press. Arbuckle was being painted as a guilty man in order to sell newspapers, but two cases brought against him were both declared mistrials after the juries became deadlocked. It did not seem to

RAPPE. — The flower-covered casket containing the body of Miss Virginia
death is the basis of the manslaughter charge against Roscoe Arbuckle, being
se for the funeral at Hollywood, California. A large crowd gathered.

CENTURY OF SCANDAL SILVER SCREEN

# THE SEVEN LEAN YEARS:

By LORD ROTHERMERE IN THE "SUNDAY PICTORIAL"

# The Daily Mirror

NET SALE NEARLY TWICE THAT OF ANY OTHER DAILY PICTURE NEWSPAPER

No. 5,591.    Registered at the G.P.O. as a Newspaper.    SATURDAY, OCTOBER 1, 1921    One Penny.

## "FATTY" ARBUCKLE ON HIS TRIAL: FIRST PICTURES

Roscoe Arbuckle (x) in court. Dominguez, his solicitor, and Brady, prosecuting, are at the table.

Miss Jeanne Dolly Clark, present at the revel, was a witness.

Miss Joyce Clark, one of the witnesses in the case.

Arbuckle questioned in the office of the Federal Prohibition Director at San Francisco concerning liquor served in his rooms.

Mrs. Bambina Maude Delmont, a friend of the deceased actress. She was present at the party and swore the complaint.

Miss Zay Prevost, an important witness, who entered the room with Mrs. Delmont and discovered Miss Rappe.

Henry Lehrman, a film producer, was Miss Rappe's fiancé. He sent a message to be whispered in her ear.

First pictures of the trial of Roscoe ("Fatty") Arbuckle, the world-famous film comedian, just received from San Francisco. After being confined for eighteen days on a charge in connection with the death of Miss Virginia Rappe, a film actress, who died after being taken ill during a party in Arbuckle's rooms, the actor has been released on bail of £1,250. The charge of manslaughter is still hanging over him, but Judge Lazarus has refused to entertain the suggestion of murder, saying that evidence produced was insufficient. "In a sense we are trying ourselves, our morals and present-day social standards," said the Judge, "a question larger than the guilt of this defendant."

# Party that ruined a fat star

matter that Rappe's history of promiscuity and alcohol abuse had been revealed, nor that she allegedly underwent a botched abortion just prior to the party.

By the time of his third trial, Arbuckle's films had been banned. This move seemed overzealous in retrospect, as the third and final jury cleared him of all charges and even went so far as to issue the following public apology:

"Acquittal is not enough for Roscoe Arbuckle. We feel that a great injustice has been done him ... there was not the slightest proof adduced to connect him in any way with the commission of a crime. He was manly throughout the case and told a straightforward story which we all believe. We wish him success and hope that the American people will take the judgement of fourteen men and women that Roscoe Arbuckle is entirely innocent and free from all blame."

Even though Arbuckle had been vindicated, his career never truly recovered. The trials left him penniless and homeless, and he was judged harshly for consuming alcohol during prohibition. Hollywood lifted its ban on him, but his audience was long gone.

He staged a comeback of sorts after a few years in the wilderness, first as a director under the pseudonym William Goodrich, and then again in 1933 when he was finally offered acting work again. His return to the screen did not materialize, though – he suffered a heart attack that year and passed away at the age of 46.

Sadly, many of his movies are gone for ever after having been destroyed in the wake of the 1921 controversy.

**ARBUCKLE'S SUSPENSE.** — Roscoe ("Fatty") Arbuckle, centre, has undergone a period of anxious suspense while awaiting the verdict concerning the death of Miss Virginia Rappe (portrait inset).

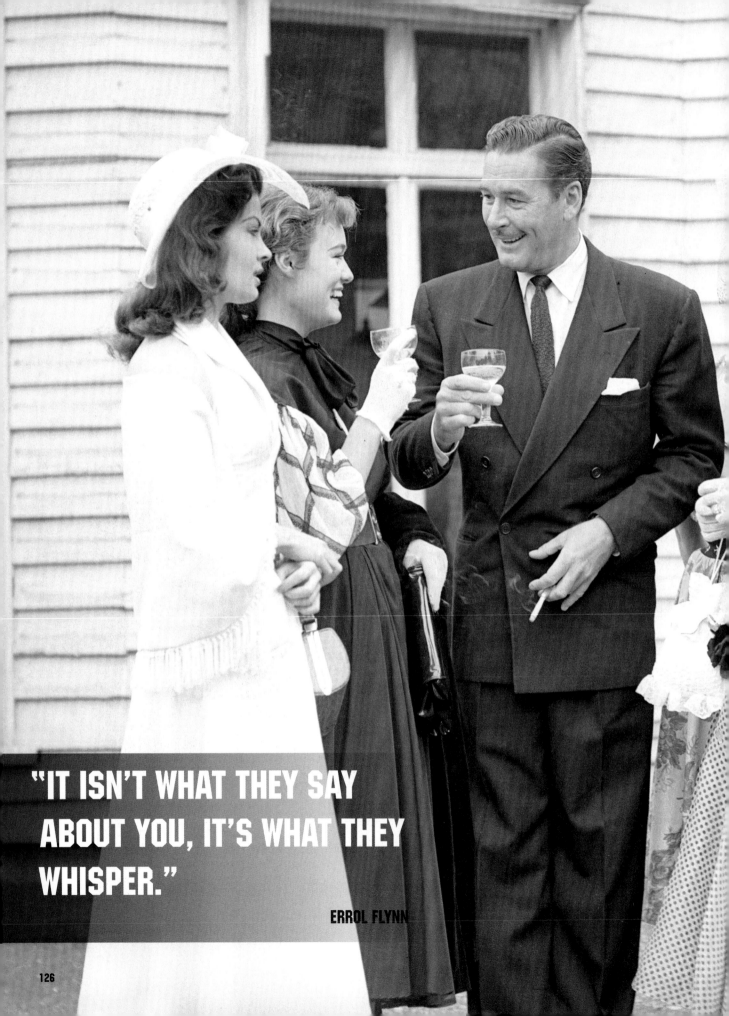

"IT ISN'T WHAT THEY SAY
ABOUT YOU, IT'S WHAT THEY
WHISPER."

ERROL FLYNN

# ERROL FLYNN

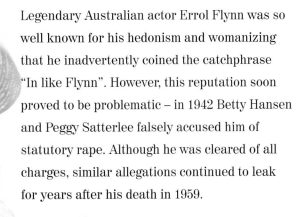

Legendary Australian actor Errol Flynn was so
well known for his hedonism and womanizing
that he inadvertently coined the catchphrase
"In like Flynn". However, this reputation soon
proved to be problematic – in 1942 Betty Hansen
and Peggy Satterlee falsely accused him of
statutory rape. Although he was cleared of all
charges, similar allegations continued to leak
for years after his death in 1959.

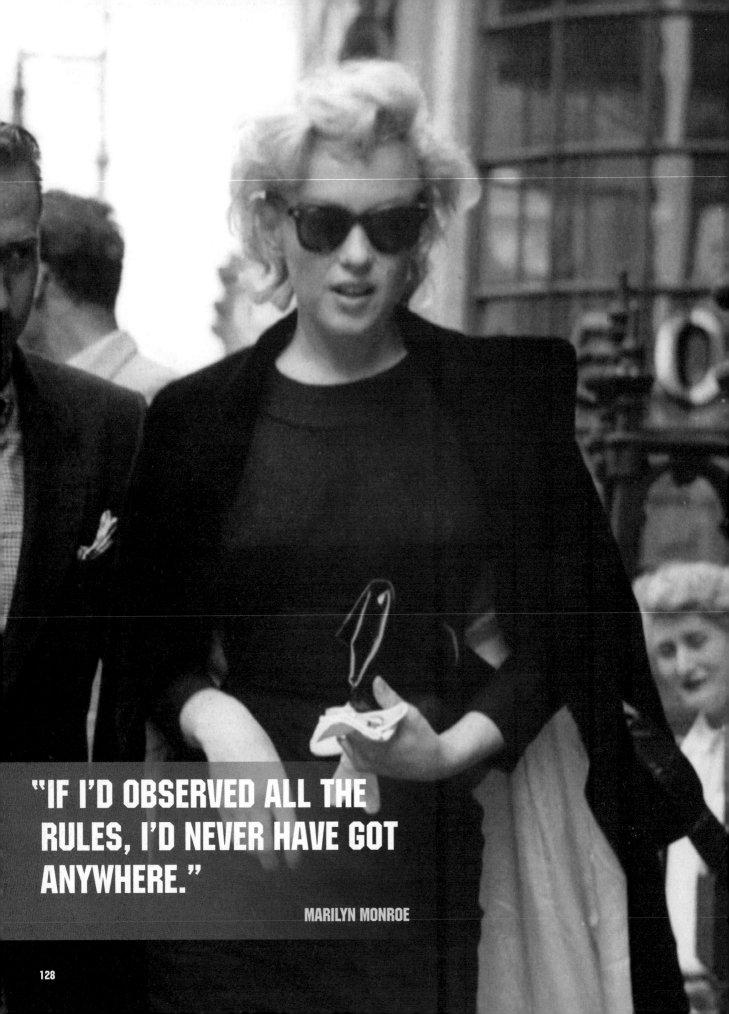

"IF I'D OBSERVED ALL THE RULES, I'D NEVER HAVE GOT ANYWHERE."

MARILYN MONROE

# MARILYN MONROE

Marilyn Monroe's tragic death remains cloaked in mystery. The 36-year-old screen siren passed away in 1962 after overdosing on barbiturates, but the coroner's ruling of "probable suicide" has been debated ever since. Although the legendary beauty was known to have struggled with drug and alcohol addiction in her final years, conspiracy theorists have claimed she was murdered as a result of her alleged association with the Kennedy brothers. Monroe famously serenaded President John F Kennedy with a unique interpretation of 'Happy Birthday' just a few months before her death, and she was rumoured to have conducted affairs with both John and his brother Bobby. If the rumours were true and she had gone public with them, the Kennedy brothers could have been ruined. Another theory regarding her death states that the mafia killed her in a bid to discredit Bobby, who was trying to crack down on organized crime at the time. Whatever

the truth of her death, it has been taken to the grave; JFK and Bobby were assassinated in 1963 and 1968 respectively.

## The last words of Marilyn Monroe

# FAREWELL TO A STAR

**DONALD ZEC** spo...

STAR TURN

# THE PROBLEM OF BEING MONROE

IN a New York hospital yesterday, the best-known and one of the most mixed-up beauties in the world was facing up to a harrowing problem — the problem of being Marilyn Monroe.

She is restless, nervous, anxious, and ill at ease. She has been taking tranquilliser pills by day, powerful sleeping pills by night.

And constantly in attendance, soothing and reassuring her, is the second husband she divorced, baseball ace Joe Di Maggio.

What is it that is driving this highly vulnerable blonde, once called "a humming-bird made of iron," to a psychiatrist's couch?

Is it because of her recently-shattered marriage to playwright Arthur Miller?

I think not. That marriage was out cold months ago, and the Hollywood-hardened Monroe recovered speedily from the blow.

Could it be grief over the sudden death of Clark Gable, her co-star on the film "The Misfits"?

Doubtful. She was upset, of course, like everyone else. But they were not close friends.

### FRAGILE

Moreover, this emotionally-battered woman, weaned on cruelty, and assaulted in her teens, knows how now to ride the punches life throws at her.

Then what is it that is disturbing the inner peace of this irresistibly-lovely creature—the most relished piece of female scenery on earth?

My guess—after some years of studying and talking with this fragile beauty—is that she is waking up to the fact that she is thirty-four years old.

BY all the ordinary rules of show business, thirty-four is still young for a star.

But Marilyn Monroe is no ordinary actress. She is the girl known to millions as "The Sex Symbol of the Age"; "The Heavenly Body radiating flashes of light: "The Most Desirable, childlike beauty in the world."

All this is fine when the bloom is still on the peach. But there comes a time when a "sex-symbol" has had its day, when the flashes from a

*At thirty-four, Marilyn is still as lovely as ever. . . . But where does she go from here?*

"heavenly body" grow dimmer, when what was "child-like" is . . . a little less so.

So many actresses, like ordinary housewives, step into their thirties and forties with a smile, if not a song.

For a sex symbol it is not so easy. Bardot must face this. Mansfield is approaching, Diana Dors is resigned to it.

But Marilyn Monroe ferociously hangs on, not giving an inch of that 38-23-36.

NO movie star in the world gives so much time, thought and money to staying as delectably beautiful as Monroe.

Wherever she goes, she takes enough lotions, potions, skin foods, paint and powders to stock a fair-sized salon.

She can dabble with Dostoievski, browse through Browning and trifle with Tennyson—but Monroe is a sexpot, and delights lu uriates, rejoices in the fact.

Dare she face the fact that behind every sex symbol is the hint

of a wrinkle and the ghost of a bulge?

While making the film "Let's Make Love" she put on excess poundage to an alarming degree. Nothing wrong with that—until you spread it across a 50-foot screen.

But Monroe, who has always regarded her bosom as a kind of treasure-chest, and her swinging hips as the movement supreme, was determined to reveal as much as she could.

Those who saw the film will concede her partial if not total victory.

THE same thing happened on "The Misfits." She wanted to appear in a bikini.

Her husband (then) Arthur Miller, who wrote the script, said there was no cause for her to wear a bikini in the picture. She persisted. Director John Huston politely supported Mr. Miller.

### CUT LOW

Still Monroe insisted. For days the wardrobe department on location in Nevada built—yes, that's the right word—a bikini for the ample Marilyn. When she relaxed it on for size, bless her, she had only one complaint. It wasn't cut low enough to suit her racy requirements.

So she had it altered and Huston shot the scene. I may add that it was a long shot and lasts only a few seconds on the screen.

Even in Nevada, with the temperature well over the hundred, she spent hours over her make-up. And always close by was her personal masseur.

On the day she arrived at Reno, a huge crowd waited to cheer her down the gangway.

Monroe kept them waiting for forty minutes. "She's in the washroom titivating her hair," explained an embarrassed air hostess.

### HAZARD

The hours that studios (and Messrs. Joe Di Maggio and Arthur Miller) have been kept hanging around for Marilyn's last-minute "facials" add up to a hell of a lot of days.

But "waiting for Marilyn" has always been the occupational hazard of those who are close to Monroe.

THE problem of this lovely, unpredictable, trouble-prone movie star is: Where does she go from here?

Highly-trained actresses, like Susan Hayward, Rita Hayworth, Bette Davis, and others, have slid gracefully into the "middle distance" of their working lives with hardly anybody noticing the change.

They have proved that lines around the eyes are no handicap to a girl with acting talent.

But can the "Sex Symbol of the Age" do the same?

Is this the problem that looms mighty big in the mind of the girl in the New York hospital?

---

**Daily Mirror**
1d. Monday, August 6, 1962      No. 18,236

**'Multi-million' star found dead in bed**

# MARILYN MONROE: 'IT LOOKS LIKE SUICIDE'

from STAR MAXS and JOHN EDWARDS New York, Sunday

MARILYN MONROE, 36-year-old Hollywood sex-symbol, was found dead in bed behind locked doors in her luxury bungalow early today.

She was slumbing a white telephone, still an its hook. On he bedside table, among thirty bottles, was an empty one which had contained sleeping pills.

The star who walled with a wiggle was called—as she always died—and remona only to a sheet and blanket.

Tonight, as her body lay in a duly bandaged Los Angeles mortuary, the at Westside Wing of the county mortuary, Coroner's officer Guy Hockett said—it looks like suicide."

Los Angeles county coroner, Dr T. Curphey, said a "device-like" suicide would determine whether or not she had died. Her death was due to natural causes or whether she had swallowed an overdose of tablets accidentally.

Marilyn's death was discovered in the middle of the night. The housekeeper at her Hollywood home, Mrs. Eunice Murray, woke up at 3 a.m. and saw the light on under Marilyn's door.

She tried the door and knocked, but could not rouse Marilyn. She called the star's personal physician, Dr Ralph Greenson, and together they woke the home.

**Stormy**

Greenson broke the bedroom window... and found Marilyn. He could not save her... and Hollywood's idol was dead.

Marilyn, the star of "The Misfits" and "Some Like It Hot," earned a fortune in her lifetime. Yet she died leaving only £73,000 and her Hollywood bungalow, the legend ended.

**HER 'WIGGLE' BECAME A LEGEND**

Millions of people throughout the world knew her just as "Marilyn." Her wiggle and her wide-eyed look

**Marriages**

The star whose marriage were in the news practically all her married life was married three times.

Her first marriage was in 1942 when she was just 16. She married James Dougherty, a young policeman. They were divorced in 1946.

Her second marriage, to baseball idol Joe Di Maggio in 1954 lasted only nine months.

Marilyn's third and last marriage was to playwright Arthur Miller in 1956. It ended in divorce in January this year.

**Come-back**

...

THE END... Coroner's officers wheel Marilyn's blanket-covered body into a Los Angeles mortuary.

---

## Heath sees Premier after '6' surprise

By WILLIAM GREIG

TALKS on Britain's entry into the six-nation Common Market gathered yesterday, day to discuss after a marathon session...

---

# Marilyn verdict leaves a mystery

... his "suicide team?" of three that Miss Monroe had aft...

"YOU FIND OUT WHO YOUR REAL FRIENDS ARE WHEN YOU'RE INVOLVED IN A SCANDAL."

ELIZABETH TAYLOR

# ELIZABETH TAYLOR

Although Oscar-winning actress Elizabeth Taylor is well known for her eight marriages, it was the two to Richard Burton that caused the most publicity.

Taylor and Burton first met in the early 1950s, but it would be another decade before their romance began. They eventually fell for one another on the set of *Cleopatra*, despite the fact that both were married at the time. According to Michael Munn's Burton biography *Prince of Players*, the actor cheated on his wife, Sybil Williams, several times – most notably with Marilyn Monroe – but Taylor was the woman to end the marriage. It was even suggested that Taylor's involvement with Burton drove Williams to attempt suicide. Meanwhile, Taylor was married to singer Eddie Fisher, who originally left *his* wife, Debbie Reynolds, to be with her. By 1964, both Taylor and Burton had sought divorces, leading the Vatican to accuse them of "erotic vagrancy".

Undeterred, the headstrong pair wed later that year, experiencing a stormy union marred by Burton's drinking and her love of drama (she later said, "I just adored fighting with Richard. I need a strong man.") When they divorced in 1974, he remarked: "You can't keep clapping a couple of dynamite sticks together without expecting them to blow up."

As it transpired, the pair couldn't bear to be apart and remarried in Botswana the following year. Their second marriage was equally doomed, lasting less than one year as a result

of Burton's continued
drinking. Despite this final split,
the legacy of their relationship
refused to die; although Taylor was
barred from Burton's funeral in 1984, she
reportedly received more condolences than his
then wife, Sally Hay.

# It's a very naughty film..

## AFTER 28 YEARS COUNCIL LIFTS BAN ON PYTHON'S LIFE OF BRIAN

**BY RICHARD SMITH**
richard.smith@mirror.co.uk

IT is a victory that will be cheered by the Judean People's Front.

Er, or was that the People's Front of Judea?

That's just one of the gags from Monty Python's comedy classic The Life of Brian that – after a 28 year wait – people in the Torbay area can at last enjoy on the big screen.

The film, a spoof of the life of Christ, was slammed by religious groups as blasphemous when it came out in 1980.

Torbay Council in South Devon was one of 28 to give it an X rating, effectively barring it at cinemas in Torquay, Paignton and Brixham.

But it has now been lifted after residents voted the film the funniest of all time in an online poll.

The area's first showing is on Sunday at the English Riviera Comedy Film Festival... at a former 12th century monastery in Torquay.

Mayor Nick Bye said: "The world has moved on. I haven't seen the film, but I welcome it."

Festival spokesman Matt Newbury said: "The humour of the ban has all the makings of a classic British comedy.

"All the decision meant was people went up the A30 to see it somewhere else."

The 1979 film stars John Cleese, Michael Palin, Terry Jones, Graham Chapman and Eric Idle and tells the story of a young Jew called Brian.

Played by Chapman, he lives in the same time as Jesus and is mistaken for the Messiah

The line "He's not the Messiah, he's a very naughty boy", spoken by Jones as Brian's mum, has been voted the funniest film line of all time.

Meanwhile, actress Sue Jones-Davies – who played Brian's girlfriend Judith – is trying to have a ban on the film lifted in Aberystwyth, Dyfed, where she is now town mayor.

But for Torbay – as the Pythons may well have said themselves: "This is an ex-X rating".

▶ THE STRIFE OF BRIAN Newspaper from 1980 reporting ban of film, left

**Torbay call for film to be banned**

# MONTY PYTHON'S LIFE OF BRIAN

Although *Monty Python's Life of Brian* was a critical and commercial success upon its release in 1979, accusations of blasphemy resulted in the religious satire being banned in certain UK towns, American states and many individual countries for over two decades.

The film's titular character exists in the same period as Jesus Christ, eventually being mistaken for the Messiah and having to deal with the unwanted attention of his over zealous "followers". *Life of Brian* culminates in a mass-crucifixion in which Brian's fellow sufferers sing 'Always Look on the Bright Side of Life', one of many scenes that provoked outrage across the world.

Despite the controversy, *Brian* went on to be recognized as one of the all-time great British film comedies, and was even screened in a Newcastle church in 2007.

# PYTHON FEELS THE SQUEEZE

# HUGH GRANT

Hugh Grant was reportedly on the verge of quitting acting when he landed the lead in 1994's *Four Weddings and a Funeral*. Despite being relatively unknown, Grant's performance opposite Andie MacDowell helped *Four Weddings* become the highest-grossing British film in history at the time, and secured his position as a bankable leading man.

The following year, Grant was in Los Angeles to promote his new comedy, *Nine Months*. Shortly before the film's release, he was arrested on Sunset Boulevard for "lewd conduct in a public place" with prostitute Divine Brown, an activity that seemed worlds away from that of the bumbling English gent he'd become famous for playing. The incident was made to seem all the more peculiar by the fact that Grant's then girlfriend, Elizabeth Hurley, was considered to be one of the most beautiful women in the world. Nobody could fathom why he had seemingly thrown everything away on a risky whim.

The American and British press had a field

# HUGH
# IDIOT

# Oh Liz..
# I've been a
# naughty boy
## HUGH BREAKS NEWS BY PHONE

day with the story, and for a moment it seemed that Grant's moment in the spotlight was up – but he defied the naysayers by honouring a scheduled appearance on the Jay Leno show. Instead of avoiding the negative publicity, Grant faced it head-on by telling the American television audience: "I think you know in life what's a good thing to do and what's a bad thing, and I did a bad thing. And there you have it." The interview was said to have saved his career.

Hurley forgave Grant, and the couple remained together until 2000. Despite Divine Brown's attempts to make as much money as possible from her newfound infamy, Grant's film career emerged unscathed.

# DIVINE GOES DOWN
## (for 30 days)

**By RICHARD WALLACE, US Editor**

HOLLYWOOD hooker Divine Brown was last night in jail after trying to lure a wealthy Las Vegas gambler into bed.

The 36-year-old, once arrested over a sex act with Hugh Grant in his car, got a 30-day sentence for soliciting a poker player who had just won £15,000.

Security guards at the MGN Grand hotel held the boozy £300-a-night prostitute after the man complained she would not take no for an answer.

A staff member said last night: "There was an unpleasant altercation.

"Ms Brown had clearly been drinking and was offering a variety of sex acts to this customer who made it plain he didn't want to know.

"But she persisted in trying to get him upstairs to his room. That's when he called for assistance. She was detained and handed over to police."

Close friend Van Banks branded mum-of-three Brown an "idiot" over her latest brush with the law.

She said: "Divine just can't help herself. The woman's got three young kids yet risks their future and her own. Now she's in prison over Christmas." Texan Brown, real name Estella Thompson, hit the headlines in June 1995 when she and Grant were charged with lewd conduct in a public place. She was jailed and fined £1,000. The actor got two years' probation and a fine of £800.

Yet while his reputation suffered, Brown later made £500,000 from TV and press interviews and porn films.

But Banks said her friend has squandered virtually every penny and added: "She's broke. That's why she's hustling her butt again."

It's the second time Brown has been arrested at the Grand. A year after her meeting with Grant she was fined £500 for soliciting two undercover policemen.

*r.wallace@mirror.co.uk*

JAILED: Brown

# WORDS OF WISDOM

"LOVE AND SCANDAL ARE THE BEST SWEETENERS OF TEA."

HENRY FIELDING (1707–1754)

# MONEY MAKES THE WORLD GO AROUND

"WE DON'T PAY TAXES. ONLY THE LITTLE PEOPLE PAY TAXES."

BILLIONAIRE HOTELIER LEONA HELMSLEY (1920–2007)

# Daily Mirror

Broadcasting - Page 20

### THE DAILY PICTURE NEWSPAPER WITH THE LARGEST NET SALE

WIFE'S SUIT:
"ENTICING
A HUSBAND"
—Page 2

No. 9,398 | Registered at the G.P.O. as a Newspaper. | TUESDAY, JANUARY 9, 1934 | One Penny

# FIGHT TO SAVE STAVISKY'S LIFE

## *Hunted Banker Shoots Himself in Villa*

## DRAMA AS DETECTIVES BATTER DOWN DOOR

**DOCTORS WERE EARLY TO-DAY FIGHTING DESPERATELY TO SAVE THE LIFE OF SERGE STAVISKY, THE HUNTED FRENCH BANKER, WHO SHOT HIMSELF AS DETECTIVES WERE BATTERING DOWN A DOOR TO ARREST HIM ON A £6,000,000 FRAUD CHARGE.**

THIS drama took place in a beautiful villa at Chamonix, the winter sports resort.

There for a week the financier had hidden while half the police of Europe, including Scotland Yard, kept a look-out for him, in vain.

### Barricaded In Room

But the net spread by M. Chiappe, the celebrated chief of the Paris police, closed relentlessly on the wanted man. False names, forged passports were of no avail. Stavisky was trapped. He barricaded himself in a bedroom. Two shots rang out . . .

When the detectives forced an entrance they found the banker in a coma on the floor—gravely injured from two bullet wounds.

He was rushed to hospital, where doctors performed a trepanning operation (removing a portion of the skull).

Through most of the night they fought to save the life of the man who did not want to live. Up to midnight he had not regained consciousness.

The news caused a sensation in Paris—a Paris already buzzing with rumours.

### Cabinet Minister Resigns

Big names were linked with the gigantic swindles. There was talk of protection from high places. The storm shook the foundations of the Government.

It was stated that M. Chautemps, the Prime Minister, had called for the resignation of M. Dalimier, the Minister for the Colonies, who is alleged to have officially recommended one of Stavisky's companies.

Then late last night it was announced that at a Cabinet Council the members unanimously declared that they recognised M. Dalimier had acted in entire good faith.

**Despite this the Minister resigned shortly afterwards.**

M. Chautemps accepted and announced: "M. Dalimier desires to regain his political liberty so that he may defend himself against unjust attacks."

Meanwhile the scandal and possible revelations are the sole topic of conversation in Paris. Several police officials are said to be involved.

(Continued on page 3)

M. Tissier, the arrested former manager of the Bayonne Crédit Municipal (or town pawnshop), leaving prison with a gendarme during the inquiries.

A recent portrait of M. Stavisky, central figure of the greatest financial scandal in France since the war.

Mme. Stavisky, who is missing from her Paris flat. The police believe that she has left for Chamonix.

A crowd outside the Bayonne Crédit Municipal after the discovery of the alleged fraud in Crédit bonds.

# THE STAVISKY AFFAIR

Alexandre Stavisky was a financier whose embezzling antics resulted in major disruption of the 1934 French government. In the late 1920s, he amassed a considerable fortune by selling valueless bonds, befriending a number of influential people along the way and becoming more flagrant in his criminal activities. He was eventually tried unsuccessfully for fraud, but by 1933 he knew his luck was running out.

Stavisky was found in early 1934 having suffered a fatal and apparently self-inflicted gunshot wound, and rumours began to surface that he had been murdered. Premier Camille Chautemps was forced to step down after his opponents claimed he had ordered Stavisky's assassination to protect ministers and other powerful figures, and his successor Édouard Daladier immediately enforced a shake-up of leading police officers and governmental figures. This caused a right-wing riot as conservative groups reacted to the new cabinet, and the violence resulted in Daladier's removal.

His replacement, Gaston Doumergue, had the unenviable task of cleaning up the mess, but the effects of *affaire Stavisky* continued to reverberate for quite some time.

CENTURY OF SCANDAL MONEY MAKES THE WORLD GO AROUND

**Daily Mirror** — THE DAILY PICTURE NEWSPAPER WITH THE LARGEST NET SALE
Broadcasting - Page 24
No. 9,436 — THURSDAY, FEBRUARY 22, 1934 — One Penny
WATER SHORTAGE: OFFICIAL WARNING

## JUDGE MURDERED TO SEAL HIS LIPS
### He Knew Too Much About Stavisky
### BODY ON RAILWAY

M. Albert Prince, who was found murdered on a railway line shortly before he was to have given evidence in connection with the Stavisky scandal.

Public Accuse High Officials of Shielding Stavisky

**Daily Mirror** — THE DAILY PICTURE NEWSPAPER WITH THE LARGEST NET SALE
Broadcasting - Page 20
No. 9,399 — WEDNESDAY, JANUARY 10, 1934 — One Penny
MYSTERY MAN KILLED IN CAR CRASH —Page 2

## STAVISKY RIOTING IN PARIS
### 250 Arrests During Dash on Parliament

### HIS BREATH HAS STOPPED, OTHERS BREATHE FREE

A demonstrator who was knocked down during last night's riots round the Paris Chamber of Deputies in connection with the Stavisky bond scandal. Over 250 arrests were made, and many people were injured.

Serge Stavisky, the shot financier, seen giving a ride to one of his children on the beach at Deauville. When Mme. Stavisky saw her husband dead in the hospital at Chamonix yesterday she collapsed at the foot of the bed, and tears poured down her cheeks.

Arrested demonstrators about to be driven away in a police wagon last night.

145

# LEONA HELMSLEY

New York hotelier and real estate guru Leona Helmsley was dubbed "Queen of Mean" by the American media, and although her tough business practices made her a billionaire, they also landed her in hot water on more than one occasion – most famously in 1989 when she went to trial for tax evasion. The case saw former maid Elizabeth Baum tell the court: "I said [to Helmsley], 'You must pay a lot of taxes.' She said, 'We don't pay taxes. Only the little people pay taxes.'" The quote was flatly denied, but Helmsley never managed to shake the negative impact of Baum's words.

Helmsley was sentenced to 16 years in jail after being convicted on various counts of conspiracy to defraud, tax evasion, filing false corporate and personal tax returns and mail fraud. Although she eventually served just 18 months before being released under house arrest, she was unable to carry on working; her

## A MEAN-spirited billionairess snubbed her grandkids in her will – while leaving $12million to her pet dog.

Bitter Leona Helmsley, dubbed "The Queen of Mean" for the way she treated staff, said Craig and Meegan Panzirer would get nothing "for reasons that are known to them".

The property mogul, who died last week at 87, is thought to have rowed with them after they failed to name any of their children after her late husband Harry. Pampered pooch

**From ANTON ANTONOWICZ in New York**

Trouble will now be the single biggest beneficiary of her £2billion fortune.

The £6million will keep Trouble in luxury and when the eight-year-old female Maltese dies she will lie next to Helmsley and her beloved Harry in a £700,000 mausoleum.

The New York tycoon's only brother Alvin Rosenthal must look after the pet but gets £1million less than it does.

The thrice-married former model

owned vast chunks of prime property, including the Empire State Building. Last year she was ranked the world's 369th richest person.

But in the 80s she was seen as a symbol of ugly corporate greed and in 1989 got 18 months for tax evasion.

The trial heard she snootily told a maid: "Only the little people pay taxes."

And in 2003 one of her staff won damages after he was sacked for being gay. Helmsley, whose only son Jay Panzirer

died of a heart attack in 1982, had four grandkids and 12 great-grandchildren. The will mentions none of her great-grandkids. However, grandsons David and Walter get £2.5million each – if they visit their dad's grave yearly.

In later years Helmsley tried to improve her tarnished name by giving millions to charities, which will now get millions more.

She also left £50,000 for her chauffeur.

*aantonowiczmirror@ gmail.com*

## RICH PETS

Dusty Springfield left cash to buy imported baby food for her cat.

● Tobacco heiress Doris Duke gave £50,000 to her four dogs.

# ..AND TO MY DOG TROUBLE I LEAVE $12M

## (but nothing for my grandkids)

CREATURE COMFORTS: Tycoon's pet

COUPLE: Helmsley and Harry

alcohol licence had been removed as part of her punishment, meaning she was unable to continue overseeing her hotel empire.

Helmsley went into retirement and was depicted as a lonely figure in her final years, passing away in 2007 from congestive heart failure. Despite this, the 87-year-old shocked America one final time by leaving $12 million to her dog, Trouble, the largest single bequest

from her estate. Two of her grandchildren received $5 million each on the proviso that they visit their grandfather's grave once a year, while another two grandchildren received nothing at all. Helmsley's will stated that this was "for reasons which are known to them," but it was later speculated that the snub came about because none of her grandchildren were named after their grandfather.

# THE £800m

## Whizz kid trader co___ll be a mega-frauds__e claims Barings boss

**RUNAWAY** dealer Nick Leeson could have deliberately sabotaged Barings bank with the help of a mystery accomplice, its chairman claimed last night.

And the men could now be cashing in on the bank's £800 million losses.

As a worldwide hunt continued for whizz kid Leeson, 28, Peter

**By KEVIN MAGUIRE**
**Industrial Editor**

Baring outlined how the alleged sting could have been carried out.

"What we are talking about here is hiding financial transactions," he said.

Mr Baring said Leeson and an unknown friend could have secretly set up loss-making deals for Barings in Singapore

which went undetected from early 1994.

Then, when the bank inevitably failed, they could have profited from the resulting falling market.

Leeson may also have been involved in financial frauds involving the Asian money markets. Informed sources

● Turn to Page 2

## STING

# NICK LEESON

The world was stunned when British trader Nick Leeson was exposed for his role in the collapse of Barings Bank. It seemed unfathomable that an overconfident 28-year-old had effectively been allowed to gamble away $1.3 billion, thereby creating a situation in which the UK's oldest investment bank was forced to declare bankruptcy. Thousands of investors subsequently lost their money, while 1,200 people found themselves unemployed as a direct result of Barings' and Leeson's mistakes.

When a catastrophic earthquake struck Kobe, Japan on 17th January 1995, Asian financial markets went into freefall. Unfortunately for Barings, Leeson had just made a significant gamble that the Japanese stock market was about to improve. This was the latest in a string of disastrous ventures by Leeson, who had been working as general manager of Barings' futures trading operation on Singapore's SIMEX since 1992. He started as a rookie talent, initially making a £10 million profit for Barings with his speculative trades – something that later appeared to have been a dramatic case of beginner's luck.

Leeson began to hide his losses in Barings' error account, and by 1994 had secretly lost over £208 million. It later transpired that Barings had allowed him to cover two posts in one – he settled his own trades despite being Chief Trader – making it easier for him to hide such colossal mistakes. The combination of Leeson's existing losses with the financial implications of the Kobe earthquake could not be ignored; Barings was confirmed as insolvent less than one month after the Kobe disaster.

Terrified of being sent to a Singapore prison, Leeson went on the run. His efforts proved fruitless, however; he was eventually arrested in Germany and extradited to Singapore, where he was sentenced to six and a half years in Changi prison. His time there was especially hard – as well as being divorced by his wife, Leeson also developed colon cancer. Despite these hardships, he managed to pen his autobiography, *Rogue Trader*, while incarcerated, and this was later turned into a film starring Ewan McGregor. Leeson was released in 1999 and successfully fought his cancer.

Although Leeson was a highly controversial figure in the mid-'90s, he has since repositioned himself as a writer and occasional public speaker. In 2007 he told the BBC that his fingers hadn't been completely burned by his experiences, saying: "I do [still] trade currencies personally, using my own money."

# GIVE UP

## EXCLUSIVE: Nick Leeson tells missing £537m rogue trader: 'Surrender pal, it's not worth it'

LOSSES: Leeson

ROGUE trader Nick Leeson last night urged the missing US banker behind a £537million fraud to give himself up.

Leeson, 35, said John Rusnak had "nowhere to run and nowhere to hide". He said: "I've been where he is.

"There's not a place on earth where he won't be found. He should give himself up immediately – it will be a blessed relief." Rusnak vanished on

**By STEPHEN MOYES**

Monday after being questioned at the weekend over money missing from Allfirst – the US arm of Allied Irish Banks – in Baltimore, Maryland.

But last night his lawyer insisted: "If they're claiming he stole money that won't pan out."

The 37-year-old father of two, described as a churchgoing "Mr Middle America", is alleged to have

bet on currency movements using false records to hide losses.

It is not known if he pocketed millions or lost the lot. The Dublin HQ of the AIB insisted the bank would survive. Boss Michael Buckley said: "It's a one-off hit. We'll deal with it."

Leeson brought down Barings Bank in 1995 after running up losses of £862million gambling on futures.

**SEE PAGES 4 & 5**

HUNTED: John Rusnak

# MARTHA STEWART

In the early 1980s, former stockbroker-turned-homemaker Martha Stewart published her bestselling cookbook, *Entertaining*. The straightforward domestic tome laid the foundations for Stewart's vast business empire, which includes multimedia, publishing and merchandising arms, as well as numerous television platforms – all of which helped consolidate her position as an

American household name.

With her wholesome image and inspiring work ethic – not to mention her millions in the bank – Stewart's legions of fans were shocked to hear that she was being investigated for security fraud and obstruction of justice. But this is precisely what happened in June 2003.

Stewart's arrest and trial had roots in the 2001 sale of her stock in medical company ImClone. ImClone had just learned that the Food and Drug Administration had refused to approve its latest product, and Stewart was one of several high-profile stockholders who managed to sell their shares before the news was made public. As ImClone's executives were questioned on suspicion of insider trading, Stewart denied any wrongdoing.

Despite her protestations, in March 2004 a jury found her guilty of conspiracy, making false statements and obstruction of justice. She was sentenced in July to five months' imprisonment followed by five months under house arrest. She told the judge: "Today is a shameful day. It is shameful for me, for my family, and for my beloved company and all of its employees and partners. What was a small personal matter became over the last two and a half years an almost fatal circus event of unprecedented proportions spreading like oil over a vast landscape. I have been choked and almost suffocated to death."

The image of America's domestic goddess behind bars was a surreal one, but Stewart appeared to bounce back from the scandal with ease. Her considerable television workload continued upon her release in March 2005, and her merchandise line was expanded to include wines and carpets.

# "WHAT WAS A SMALL PERSONAL MATTER BECAME OVER THE LAST TWO AND A HALF YEARS AN ALMOST FATAL CIRCUS EVENT OF UNPRECEDENTED PROPORTIONS SPREADING LIKE OIL OVER A VAST LANDSCAPE..."

**MARTHA STEWART**

# JOHN AND ANNE DARWIN

Nobody knew quite what to make of the news that a dead man had walked into a West End police station, but that's what happened when John Darwin appeared in December 2007 and told startled officers, "I think I am a missing person."

John was indeed a missing person, and had even been declared dead in 2003 after failing to return from a canoe expedition at sea the previous year. However, four years after the coroner's verdict, police began to look into the Darwins' unusual finances and property portfolio. As this development broke, Darwin's wife, Anne, informed her sons that she was relocating to Panama. Two months after that, John reappeared. Unluckily, a recent photograph of him and his wife had also just surfaced on the website of a Panamanian estate agent. John and Anne had been trying to open a canoeing school in the Central American republic, but the hapless fraudsters seemed to have forgotten that the World Wide Web was just that – worldwide.

Darwin was arrested on suspicion of fraud just days after returning from the dead, and police announced their intentions to question Anne. She returned from Panama under a growing cloud of suspicion and public incredulity, and was arrested on the spot. The amazing extent of their bumbling fraud began to emerge – during his five years as a "dead" man, Darwin had actually been living next door to his wife, using a secret door to move between the two houses.

Unsurprisingly, the Darwins' sons,

# WHERE WAS I FOR 5 YEARS?

**Amazing mystery of missing canoeist**

By **JEREMY ARMSTRONG**

A DAD missing for five years has no idea where he has been.

John Darwin, 57, was thought drowned off Cleveland in March 2002. Police said: "He can't remember anything about what's happened to him."

**FULL STORY: PAGES 4 & 5**

# SECRET OO LIFE OF MR CANOE

MYSTERY: Anne moved to Panama weeks before John came back

## EXCLUSIVE
### From DAVID LEIGH in Panama City

THE wife of missing canoeist John Darwin said last night: "I can't believe he is back from the dead after five years."

But Anne Darwin, 55 – who moved to Panama City six weeks ago – is in no hurry to return to the UK to see John, 57. She said: "There are a few things I need to sort out here first."

John, thought drowned off Cleveland in 2002, may have spent the years since in America with a woman he met on the internet. Last night he said he couldn't remember anything since June 2000.

**FULL STORY: PAGES 4 & 5**

who were cleared of any involvement, announced they wanted nothing more to do with their parents, telling the press they were "victims of a scam" and that they had believed their father was dead.

John and Anne were each sentenced to just over six years in prison on fraud charges, and are rumoured to be planning a tell-all book of their various crimes.

# CANOE MAN AND WIFE REUNITED.. IN THE DOCK

Couple face more charges over 'scam'

ACCUSED: Anne and John Darwin

**By JEREMY ARMSTRONG**

CANOE man John Darwin will see his wife today for the first time since he reappeared, standing beside her in the dock.

Darwin, 57, and wife Anne, 55, will face more charges over his disappearance – understood to be obtaining £200,000 by deception.

He is already accused of obtaining £25,000 in relation to a fatal accident policy and making a false passport application, both in 2003.

His wife will also face further charges when they appear before Hartlepool magistrates.

She is already accused of obtaining £162,000 by deception in relation to insurance and mortgage policies and Darwin's pension after he vanished. The couple were

taken from their jail cells yesterday to Kirkleatham police station, North Yorks.

They were questioned by detectives investigating payouts for their property, insurance policies and Darwin's pension after he vanished.

His solicitor John Nixon said

last night: "He did not get to see his wife when they were questioned but it is my understanding that they will appear together in court."

The wife's solicitor Nicola Finnerty said: "I can only confirm that she has been interviewed by police and is

due before the court to face further charges."

It was the couple's 34th wedding anniversary three days before Christmas.

Darwin, held in Durham jail, begged authorities to let him see his wife – who is four miles away in Low Newton Remand

Centre – over Christmas but was refused.

The ex-prison officer disappeared from his home in Seaton Carew, Co Durham, in March 2002 and was presumed drowned after his wrecked canoe was found weeks later on the shore.

He last saw his wife in Panama City on November 28 last year when he flew back to London, handing himself to police on December 1 saying: "I think I'm a missing person."

His wife claimed she was in "total shock" that he was alive.

But the Mirror confronted her with an internet photo of them together in Panama in July 2006 and she admitted he had been living next door to their home from February 2003.

Sons Anthony, 32, and Mark, 29, have disowned them both. Police said the men are victims of the couple's alleged scam.

*jeremy.armstrong@mirror.co.uk*

# WORDS OF WISDOM

"A LIE HAS NO LEG, BUT A SCANDAL HAS WINGS."

THOMAS FULLER (1608–1661)

# WHAT'S MINE IS YOURS

"THE ONLY SOLID AND LASTING PEACE BETWEEN A MAN AND HIS WIFE IS, DOUBTLESS, A SEPARATION."

LORD CHESTERFIELD, BRISITH STATESMAN, AUTHOR (1694-1773)

High-profile marriages are famous for ending hastily or acrimoniously – and in countless cases, both. Many a millionaire has been ordered to hand a sizeable chunk of change to their former partner, a phenomenon that has helped turn "prenuptial agreement" into an everyday household phrase. Shockingly expensive divorces of recent times include:

## JOHN CLEESE AND ALYCE FAYE EICHELBERGE

It was a case of third time unlucky for writer, actor and comedian John Cleese when his 16-year marriage to third wife Alyce collapsed

in 2008. She was awarded £8 million in cash, a multi-million pound property portfolio and £600,000 a year for seven years. The ruling left her richer than him.

## MICK JAGGER AND JERRY HALL

Jerry Hall was Mick Jagger's second wife – the Rolling Stone was still married to his first, Bianca Jagger, when they began dating. Jagger and Hall married in Indonesia in 1990, eventually splitting in 1999 after it was revealed that Jagger was expecting a child with model Luciana Gimenez. Hall demanded a divorce, but

Jagger claimed that their "Hindu wedding" was unofficial. He eventually handed over a reported £12 million of his £215-million fortune.

## SIR PAUL McCARTNEY AND HEATHER MILLS

In 2008, former Beatle Sir Paul McCartney became locked in a bitter legal battle with wife Heather when she demanded £125 million of his £400-million estate. In the end she walked away with £16.5 million cash and assets totalling £7.8 million. She celebrated by throwing a carafe of water over McCartney's lawyer, Fiona Shackleton.

## PHIL COLLINS AND ORIANNE CEVEY

Solo star and Genesis frontman Phil Collins topped McCartney's £24.3 million to Heather Mills when he gave £25 million to ex-wife

BELOW: Phil
Collins.

Orianne Cevey in 2008. The pair were married for seven years and had two children together. In comparison, his previous divorce in 1994 cost a trifling £17 million.

## MICHAEL AND DIANDRA DOUGLAS

Before Michael Douglas was free to marry Catherine Zeta Jones, he had to pay a whopping $40 million to wife of 22 years, Diandra. The 1997 settlement was almost a third of his $150-million fortune.

## RAY AND KAREN PARLOUR

Karen Parlour made the headlines in 2004 when a judge awarded her a substantial

**LANDMARK DIVORCE PAYOUT**

# HE SHOOTS SHE SCORES

**WHAT KAREN GETS FROM £1.2M RAY**

WINNER: Karen got her share

**£406,500** a year for 4 years

**2 houses** worth over £1M

Karen Parlour
7th July 2004
£250,000
Two hundred and fifty thousand pounds

**£250,000** lump sum payment PLUS £12,500 a year each to bring up their three children

STAR: Ray Parlour on the pitch

cut of her footballer husband's future earnings. Her settlement included £406,500 a year for a minimum of four years, two mortgage-free houses worth over £1 million each, £250,000 in cash, £12,500 a year for each of their three children, plus a third of her ex-husband's £1.2-million annual salary.

**ABOVE:** Michael Douglas.

**LEFT:** Ray and Karen Parlour.

**ABOVE:** Harrison
Ford.

LEFT: Tom Cruise and Nicole Kidman.

BELOW: Steven Spielberg.

## HARRISON FORD AND MELISSA MATHISON

Harrison Ford's 2004 divorce from Melissa Mathison cost him a cool $50 million, one of Hollywood's highest settlements…

## TOM CRUISE AND NICOLE KIDMAN

… Beating Tom Cruise and Nicole Kidman's alleged $46 million split in 2001…

## STEVEN SPIELBERG AND AMY IRVING

… But failing to match the eye-watering $100 million won by Amy Irving after her 1989 divorce from director Steven Spielberg. Don't feel too sorry for him though – his net worth is said to be around $3.1 billion.

## MADONNA AND GUY RITCHIE

Once again proving that she can hold her own against the boys, in 2008 Madonna became one of the few high-profile women to hand over the cash to her (ex) man. Her director husband Guy Ritchie reportedly received between £50 million and £60 million after their split.

## ANNE ROBINSON AND JOHN PENROSE

British TV institution Anne Robinson lost £20 million after splitting from her husband John Penrose in 2007. The pair had been married for 27 years.

## NEIL DIAMOND AND MARCIA MURPHEY

Crooner Neil Diamond handed half of his £150-million piggy bank to ex-wife Marcia Murphey in 1995, remarking afterwards that she was "worth every penny".

## JOHN AND BEVERLEY CHAPMAN

Britain's biggest ever divorce payout went to Beverley Chapman, ex-wife of London stockbroker John Chapman. In 2006, she was awarded £48 million of his riches.

## MICHAEL AND JUANITA JORDAN

It was a slam-dunk for Juanita Jordan when a judge awarded her $168 million of her husband Michael's fortune in 2007.

## ADNAN AND SORAYA KHASHOGGI

All these divorces pale in comparison to the Khashoggi divorce of 1980. Billionaire Turkish-Saudi Arabian arms dealer Adnan had to pay £500 million to his former beloved, Soraya.

**ABOVE:** Neil Diamond.

**FAR LEFT:** Madonna and Guy.

**TOP LEFT:** Anne Robinson and ex-husband John Penrose.

WORDS OF WISDOM

"THINK HOW MANY BLAMELESS LIVES ARE BRIGHTENED BY THE BLAZING INDISCRETIONS OF OTHER PEOPLE."

SAKI

# THIS SPORTING LIFE

**ORTS GOODS**

PHONE 23694

"I DON'T BELIEVE
PROFESSIONAL ATHLETES
SHOULD BE ROLE MODELS."

CHARLES BARKLEY, RETIRED BASKETBALL STAR

# CROWHURST TALKED OF SUCCESS.. AND DEATH

# DONALD CROWHURST

When amateur sailor Donald Crowhurst learned that the *Sunday Times* was staging a non-stop, round-the-world yacht race, he thought he had found the answer to his financial problems. He planned to complete the trip with the aid of navigational and safety devices he had invented, and then market the equipment to like-minded enthusiasts upon his return. Sadly, he was woefully underprepared for such an undertaking and ran into trouble almost immediately.

According to Crowhurst's logbook, his initial speeds were half of what he had predicted, and within weeks he realized he was unlikely to complete the voyage. To make matters worse, he had not completed work on his various devices and was locked in a futile bid to finish them as he sailed. The situation was dire and he was running out of options – returning would mean financial ruin and humiliation, carrying on could mean death. The stress caused Crowhurst to concoct a new plan: he would remain in the South Atlantic for several months and rejoin the race at an appropriate time. To make the ruse believable, he began to falsify his logbooks and send deliberately vague radio transmissions regarding his whereabouts.

The plan began to unravel when he heard that a competitor had dropped out of the race.

Meanwhile, the sailor Robin Knox-Johnston had already finished, meaning that Crowhurst and fellow entrant Nigel Tetley appeared to be in the running for second place. In reality, Tetley was way ahead – but news of Crowhurst's faked location panicked him. In an attempt to gain the lead, Tetley's boat collapsed under pressure, meaning Crowhurst became the sole remaining contestant. His plan was in ruins – having intended to finish last and therefore avoid suspicion, Crowhurst was now about to take second place. This would mean his falsified logbooks would be carefully scrutinized and the fraud inevitably exposed.

The last radio transmission from Crowhurst was received on 29th July 1969. He made one more log entry before his empty boat was discovered on 10th July. Close examination of his remaining logbooks suggested that Crowhurst had almost certainly suffered a mental breakdown and committed suicide by leaping overboard, as there were no signs that a storm or large wave could have claimed his life.

The story resulted in a media frenzy, causing Knox-Johnston to donate his winnings to Crowhurst's devastated widow and children. His ill-fated Teignmouth Electron boat was sold several times and now lies in ruins on the Caribbean island of Cayman Brac.

# LONE SAILOR FEARED DEAD

# SHERGAR

Shergar was a champion racehorse who galloped into public affection after winning the 1981 Derby by a record 10 lengths. His racing prowess made him an extremely valuable stud, and Lloyds of London valued him at £10 million, a figure that prompted a wealthy consortium to snap up 40 shares in him at £250,000 each. His worth had not gone unnoticed by less desirable types, however, and in 1983 he was kidnapped in Ireland by at least six masked gunmen.

The well-organized intruders stole Shergar the day before a large racehorse sale, so his horsebox went unnoticed among the hordes of similar vehicles moving around Ireland at the time. Despite this setback, a nationwide investigation commenced and secret negotiations with the kidnappers got under way. They mistakenly believed that Islamic leader the Aga Khan was Shergar's sole owner, but in fact he held just six shares in the horse. The remaining members of the syndicate collectively refused to meet ransom demands over fears this would turn other racehorses into targets, and the

## SHERGAR £2m ransom riddle

KIDNAPPED racehorse Shergar was the centre of a £2 million ransom mystery last night.

An armed gang who stole Shergar, winner of the 1981 Derby from the Aga Khan's Irish stud on Tuesday night, told a captive groom at the time that they would be demanding £2 million for his safe return.

They promised more details at noon yesterday. But last night, more than 24 hours after the raid, they had made no contact.

Police were checking on reports that a car and horsebox were seen heading towards the Ulster border at dawn yesterday.

But detectives admitted they know nothing yet about the gang. The man leading the hunt said: "I do not believe any ransom will be paid, and police will block any attempt to pay one."

● The Wonder Horse—Pages 2 and 3

# Shergar: Is he alive or dead?

kidnappers began to realize that their plan had been thwarted.

A widely accepted theory began to circulate that the IRA masterminded Shergar's capture in order to raise money for arms, and former IRA man Sean O'Callaghan later claimed that the horse panicked and injured himself shortly after being snatched. O'Callaghan went on to say that the kidnappers had been unprepared for such a reaction and were forced to kill Shergar before burying him in an unmarked grave.

Although Shergar's remains have never been found, in 2008 a source told the *Sunday Telegraph* that the kidnappers had machine-gunned Shergar to death after police surveillance hampered their efforts to move or release him. Tragically, this would have been a painful and pointless end for Shergar, as nobody appears to have benefited from his abduction – most insurers refused to pay out to shareholders because there was no proof of death.

# THE WONDER HORSE

## The syndicate who stand to lose so much

# MIKE TYSON

When boxer Mike Tyson was declared "undisputed champion" at the end of the 1980s, his personal life went off the rails. His marriage to Robin Givens broke down, and in 1992 he was found guilty of raping 18-year-old Desiree Washington. He was sentenced to six years in prison and four years probation, but was released after three and allowed to resume his boxing career. He was involved in a second major scandal in 1997 when he bit off part of opponent Evander Holyfield's ear during a well publicized re-match. The savage attack almost landed him back in prison, but Tyson escaped with a $3-million fine and a temporary boxing ban from the Nevada State Athletic Commission.

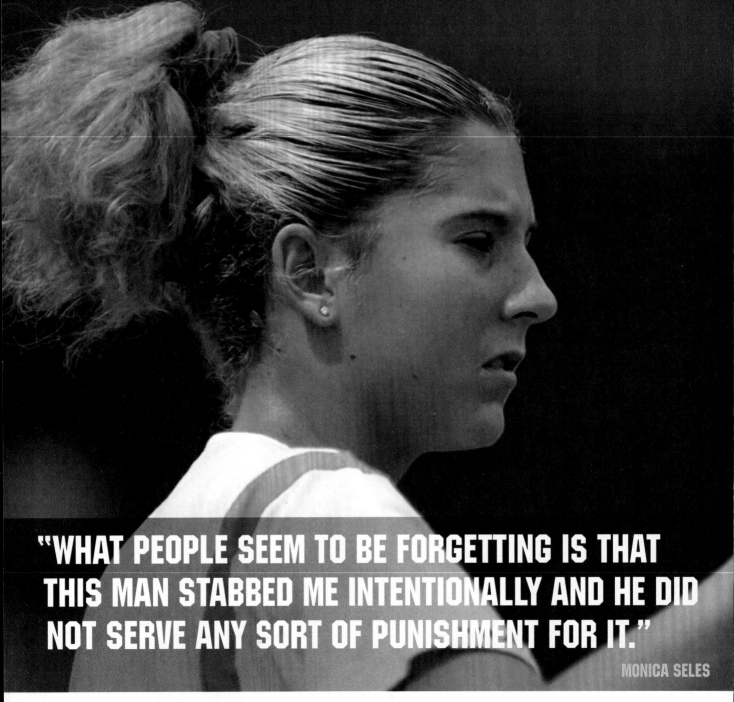

"WHAT PEOPLE SEEM TO BE FORGETTING IS THAT THIS MAN STABBED ME INTENTIONALLY AND HE DID NOT SERVE ANY SORT OF PUNISHMENT FOR IT."

MONICA SELES

# MONICA SELES

Despite retiring in 2008 at the age of 34, tennis player Monica Seles still holds the record for most Grand Slam singles titles won as a

teenager – eight before the age of 20 – and is considered one of the greatest players of all time. But a scandalous attack in 1993 undoubtedly prevented her from reaching her true potential.

On 30th April 1993, 19-year-old Seles was beating Magdalena Maleeva in a quarter-final match in Hamburg, Germany. During a break in the game, she sat with her back to the crowd as

# Champ is stabbed on court

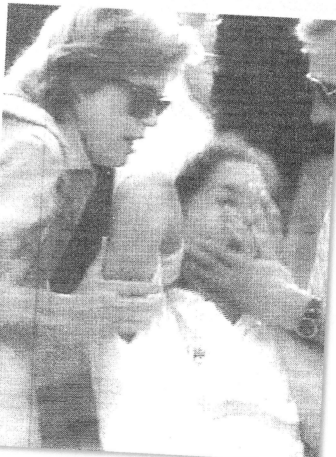

usual. Without warning, 38-year-old Günter Parche ran from the crowd and leapt onto the court before plunging a long kitchen knife directly between Seles' shoulder blades. She screamed, clutched her back, and fell to the ground in full view of stunned spectators.

Seles was immediately taken to hospital and told she was "lucky". Although the blade penetrated to a depth of 1.5 cm, doctors revealed that the attack could easily have paralysed her. She recovered in a matter of weeks, but the psychological scars ran deeper – it would be two years before she returned to

# Knifeman missed Monica's spinal cord by a whisker

professional tennis.

In the aftermath of the event, some theorized that the attack was politically motivated because of Seles' Serbian roots. It later transpired, however, that Parche was a mentally disturbed man who was obsessed with Steffi Graf. He claimed he was attempting to help Graf get back on top of her game by "removing" Seles, an explanation which ultimately prevented him from receiving a custodial sentence. Despite admitting the attack was premeditated, Parche was not charged with attempted murder. Instead, he faced a lesser charge of wounding, and his prolonged trial finally came to an end after reports concluded that he required psychological counselling and two years' probation. Seles tried to sue the German Tennis Federation for a lack of security and subsequent loss of income, but lost both cases.

Seemingly abandoned by the courts and betrayed by her peers – when given the option of keeping Seles' number one title until her condition was clarified, only Gabriela Sabatini voted "yes" – Seles felt dejected. She refused to play in Germany again, saying: "What people seem to be forgetting is that this man stabbed me intentionally and he did not serve any sort of punishment for it... I would not feel comfortable going back. I don't foresee that happening." Many years later, she explained to the *Guardian*: "It felt like everyone benefited from the stabbing except me... They just wanted me to go away, it felt like... I was 19 years old. Their money was tied up to the ranking system, and that was obviously an issue."

Although Seles staged a comeback from 1995 onwards, she was unable to reach the consistent level she had previously achieved. Her coach father was diagnosed with terminal cancer and she was criticized for putting on weight, while a new haircut was deemed unflattering and masculine. In addition to these stresses, her notorious "grunting" during play was receiving complaints. Seles managed one more Grand Slam win – the 1996 Australian Open – before continuing with varying degrees of success until 2002. A foot injury prevented her from joining the 2003 French Open, and she did not play in any more official tours.

Seles netted almost $15 million in prize money during her turbulent career, but as *Sports Illustrated* writer Jon Wertheim noted, it is her dignity that she will be remembered for. "Transformed from champion to tragedienne," he wrote, "Seles became far more popular than she was while winning all those titles. It became impossible to root against her. At first, out of sympathy. Then, because she revealed herself to be so thoroughly thoughtful, graceful, dignified. When she quietly announced her retirement... she exited as perhaps the most adored figure in the sport's history. As happy endings go, one could do worse."

# TONYA HARDING

American figure skating became an unlikely *cause célèbre* in 1994 when champion skater Tonya Harding was accused of being involved

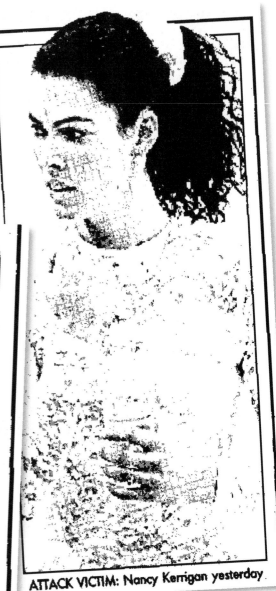

ATTACK VICTIM: Nancy Kerrigan yesterday

## Skater Tonya repents sins

SKATING ace Tonya Harding went to church on the eve of her departure for the Winter Olympics in Norway to publicly repent her sins. Tonya, 23, knelt before a pastor as he led her through a prayer for sinners.

She has admitted she found out about the attack on rival Nancy Kerrigan soon after it happened, but did not report it to the police.

Her husband, Jeff Gillooly, a bodyguard and two other men have already been charged with the iron-bar assault.

Tonya attended the First Church of the Nazarene in Portland, Oregon yesterday.

And the Rev Gary Henecke said: "She said she wanted to receive Christ as her personal saviour and wanted a prayer for the forgiveness of sins."

Tonya, who could be disciplined by the US Olympics Committee after the games, has been offered £175,000 from Playboy to pose for them.

PRAYING: Tonya

with an assault that left rival Nancy Kerrigan with knee injuries.

It soon came to light that Kerrigan's assailant Shane Stant had been hired by Harding's ex-husband Jeff Gillooly and her bodyguard Shawn Eckhardt. Kerrigan's injuries forced her to pull out of the US Figure Skating Championships, which Harding went on to win. Harding eventually admitted that she had helped to cover up the attack on Kerrigan, and an Olympic Committee

# Shamed skater Tonya back with a crash

BACK DOWN TO EARTH: Tonya fell twice during her controversial return to skating. Inset, she clings unhappily to her mascot, Lucky

DISGRACED ice skater Tonya Harding's return to the rink ended in tears yesterday when she fell twice.

She looked ready to throttle her fluffy leopard mascot, Lucky, after he failed to save her from two crashing falls. Harding, 29,

From ANDY LINES in New York

was barred for life from skating for her involvement in a baseball bat attack on sports rival Nancy Kerrigan.

But she got round the ruling by taking part in a professional skating championship which is not covered by the ban.

Empty seats outnumbered spectators for the contest staged at Huntington Beach, West Virginia.

Harding ended up fourth out of five. She said afterwards: "I was very nervous. I had not skated in front of an audience since the 1994 Olympics."

Harding's ex-husband, Jeff Gillooly, was jailed for whacking Nancy Kerrigan on the knee during a training session before the '94 Olympics.

tried unsuccessfully to remove her from the forthcoming Winter Games.

In February 1994, Harding and Kerrigan found themselves in the awkward position of having to practise together under the watchful eye of the world's media, but this time it was Kerrigan who had the last laugh. Having recovered from her injuries, she won Olympic silver while Harding had to make do with eighth place.

Gillooly went to trial for his role in Kerrigan's assault, and as part of a plea bargain he testified against Harding. She escaped jail by pleading guilty to hindering the investigation and was sentenced to three years' probation, 500 hours of community service and a $110,000 fine. She was also stripped of her title by the United States Figure Skating Association and banned for life from competing in or coaching at further events.

"I HAVE ALWAYS WANTED TO
BE LIKED AND RESPECTED."

O.J. SIMPSON

# O.J. SIMPSON

Orenthal James "O.J." Simpson was one of America's most popular sportsmen when he retired from professional football in 1979. His twilight years were expected to be relaxed, happy and lucrative, as the National Football League star had already embarked upon a successful film career even before announcing his exit from the game. He also found success as a sports commentator and businessman, as well as endorsing brands such as Wilson Sporting Goods and car hire firm Hertz.

All seemed to be going well for O.J., who was inducted into the Pro Football Hall of Fame in 1985, the same year his glamorous wife Nicole Simpson gave birth to their first child, daughter Sydney. 1988 saw the birth of a second child, Justin, as well as O.J.'s first

appearance as Detective Nordberg in the first of three *Naked Gun* comedies – arguably his best-known film role.

Despite these achievements, O.J.'s popularity was about to come crashing down in a scandal that gripped America. On 13th June 1994, the mutilated bodies of his now ex-wife Nicole and her friend Ronald Goldman were discovered outside her home by concerned neighbours. Five days later, O.J. was arrested and charged with both murders, signalling the beginning of the most publicized murder trial in American history.

## TIMELINE

**1977:** O.J. Simpson meets waitress Nicole Brown for the first time.

**1980:** Simpson divorces first wife Marguerite.

**1985:** Simpson marries Brown in a summer wedding. A daughter, Sydney, is born later that year.

**1988:** Simpson and Brown welcome a son, Justin, into the world.

**1989:** Simpson pleads no contest to spousal abuse. In his later murder trial, prosecuting lawyer Christopher Darden argued that police could not have been trying to "frame" O.J. as they were called to his house eight times in 1989 before finally arresting him for domestic assault.

**1992:** Brown files for divorce, citing "irreconcilable differences".

**1994:** 13th **June** – In the early hours of the

# MURDER CHARGE O.J. ON THE RUN

morning, the howling of Brown's dog alerts concerned neighbours. It is found with bloodied paws, and the mutilated bodies of Brown and her friend Ronald Goodman are discovered outside her condominium. Brown's injuries are so severe that she has almost been decapitated, while Goodman's body displays signs of "teaser wounds", indicating that he was initially tortured with smaller stabs. Police detective Mark Fuhrman visits Simpson's house only to find he has flown to Chicago on business. Fuhrman notices blood on the driveway and finds a bloodied leather glove.

Sydney and Justin Simpson are later revealed to have been asleep inside at the time of the murders, which occurred between 10.15pm and 10.40pm the previous evening.

**17th June** – Having failed to hand himself in for questioning, Simpson becomes involved in a low-speed car chase with police. The pursuit is televised live and watched by millions, with Simpson reportedly holding a loaded gun to his head throughout. The 35mph "chase" comes to an end at 8pm at Simpson's house, at which point he is finally taken in for questioning.

**21st June** – A jury is assembled to decide whether Simpson can be charged over the double homicide, but a series of media intrusions results in the unreliable panel being dismissed.

**7th July** – A judge announces there is enough evidence to proceed with a case against Simpson.

**23rd July** – Simpson claims he is "absolutely, one hundred percent, not guilty".

**1995: 25th January** – Simpson's televised trial for double homicide begins. It lasts for 134 days, involves 150 witnesses, and is later noted for being the longest trial in Californian history. The court transcript eventually runs to over 50,000 pages.

Despite the lack of a murder weapon or witness to the murders, the prosecution was confident of a conviction based on seemingly overwhelming DNA evidence. Simpson's history of domestic violence was also raised, though the defence argued that few abusive men end up murdering their partner.

**16th May** – A DNA expert testifies that blood found on the leather glove at Simpson's house belonged to Goldman. The matching glove was found at the murder scene.

Simpson's crack team of defence lawyers later argued that police incompetence led to contaminated DNA; a police assistant was said to have handled blood from the murder scene incorrectly.

**15th June** – Simpson, already wearing a rubber glove so as not to contaminate the evidence, tries the leather glove on in court. It does not fit, though it is later claimed the glove has been repeatedly frozen and dethawed during the DNA-testing process, a procedure that may have affected its shape. Simpson is also said to have stopped taking his arthritis medicine, potentially causing his hands to swell in court.

# WE'LL KILL O.J.

# I'M NOT SURPRISED THEY THINK I DID IT

**22nd June** – Prosecutors argue that Simpson's blood was found at the crime scene because of cuts to his hand suffered during the attack on Goldman. The defence counter-argues that there were no correlating cuts on the gloves, and that police detective Mark Fuhrman may have planted the glove found at Simpson's property.

Fuhrman's integrity was called into question after he was charged with perjury during the trial. Simpson's lawyers successfully proved Fuhrman had lied when he denied under cross-examination that he used the word "nigger" within 10 years of the Simpson trial.

**3rd October** – More than half of all Americans tune in to see a jury return Simpson's "not guilty" verdict. Public opinion is divided. Polls indicate that most black Americans perceive Simpson to be a victim of institutionalized racism, while more than 50% of white Americans believe he is guilty.

**1996:** Sydney and Justin Simpson, who stayed with their maternal grandparents during the murder trial, are returned into Simpson's care by court order.

**1997:** **5th February** – Simpson is found liable for the wrongful deaths of Goldman and Brown in a civil trial brought by Goldman's family. He is ordered to pay $33.5 million dollars in compensation, but his considerable NFL pension is exempt from being used in such circumstances. He never comes close to paying the full amount.

**2006:** *National Enquirer* announces the imminent release of Simpson's *If I Did It* book, stating that it will be a "hypothetical confession". Although 400,000 copies are printed, the project is shelved in the face of a huge public outcry.

**2007:** The bizarre tome is eventually published under the new name *If I Did It: Confessions of the Killer* with additional notes from the Goldman family and the book's ghostwriter, Pablo Fenjves. Profits are redirected to the Goldmans with the intention of reclaiming some of the compensation still owed to them.

**13th September** – Simpson becomes embroiled in a fresh scandal after being caught stealing sports memorabilia from a Las Vegas hotel room.

**16th September** – Simpson is arrested but insists he was recovering items that rightfully belonged to him.

**2008:** **15th September** – Simpson's trial begins.

**3rd October** – Precisely 13 years after his acquittal of the murders of Nicole Brown and

Ronald Goldman, Simpson is found guilty of all 12 charges relating to the Vegas robbery, including kidnap and robbery and assault with a deadly weapon.

**5th December** – Simpson is sentenced to 33 years in prison with a minimum period of nine years served.

# Clues that proved Simpson had lied

# BEST'S FIGHT FOR LIFE

## GEORGE BEST

George Best's prodigious football skill made him a legend, but his controversial lifestyle away from the pitch can never be forgotten. In the 1970s his riotous behaviour became as notorious as his playing, and it wasn't long before Best was in the grip of alcoholism. 1984 saw him slapped with a three-month jail term for drink-driving, and in 1990 he stunned viewers of Terry Wogan's chat show by appearing inebriated on live television and declaring, "I like screwing, alright?"

Best's drinking became so extreme that he required a liver transplant in 2002, but he disappointed doctors by continuing to drink after the operation. His body was not strong enough to handle the relapse, and Best fell seriously ill with kidney and lung infections. He asked to be photographed on his deathbed, and the distressing picture appeared in a tabloid alongside the headline "Don't die like me". He passed away on 20th November 2005, aged 59.

## George in hospital after liver scare

ORDEAL: Soccer hero George had stomach pains

**SOCCER** legend George Best was in hospital last night after suffering severe stomach pains.

He has suspected liver problems and doctors have warned heavy boozer Best: "Your drinking could kill you."

His wife Alex, 27, told friends she was "very concerned". Now Best faces an

---

**By LUCY ROCK, JAMES FLETCHER and PHILIP NETTLETON**

---

agonising battle to save himself. His body has turned yellow which could be jaundice — a sign of cirrhosis of the liver which kills 2,500 a year.

Medics say Best, 53, can only recover

**TURN TO PAGE 7**

# WORDS OF WISDOM

"THERE IS SO MUCH GOOD IN THE WORST OF US, AND SO MUCH BAD IN THE BEST OF US, THAT IT HARDLY BECOMES ANY ONE OF US TO TALK ABOUT THE REST OF US."

ANON

# SEX, DRUGS & ROCK 'N' ROLL

## "WE'RE MORE POPULAR THAN JESUS NOW."

**JOHN LENNON**

# SEX PISTOLS

British punk band Sex Pistols based their entire career on controversy. Formed as a disenchanted reaction to the peace and love movement of the 1960s, Sex Pistols managed to shock and offend just about everybody during their initial two and a half years in the spotlight. Here is a timeline of their most notorious moments.

## August 1975

John Lydon successfully auditions to become the Sex Pistols singer. Later rechristened Johnny Rotten on account of his bad breath.

## February 1976

The group's London Marquee gig becomes their first significant live performance, with Rotten

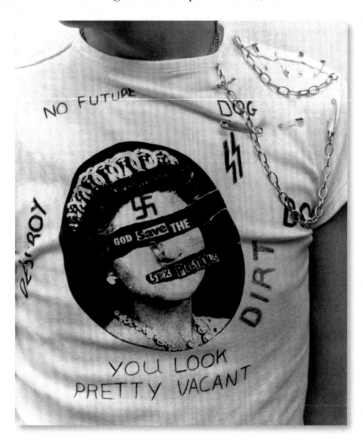

trashing equipment and abusing the audience. Sex Pistols' reputation for violent concerts is born.

## October 1976

Sex Pistols sign with EMI. A single, 'Anarchy In The UK', is released the following month.

## December 1976

The band swears repeatedly during a live broadcast of the *Today* programme. Host Bill Grundy goads them into saying something outrageous and is called a "f***ing rotter" in return. The ensuing media storm cements Sex Pistols' notoriety and results in Grundy losing his job.

## January 1977

EMI release the band from their contract over fears they are too controversial.

## February 1977

Bass player Glen Matlock quits the band. Sid Vicious, who does not know how to play and comes with a violent reputation, replaces him.

## March 1977

The group sign with A&M during a staged photo shoot outside Buckingham Palace. Their violent behaviour in the label's offices results in the contract being terminated almost immediately. Initial pressings of their planned 'God Save The Queen' single are destroyed.

## May 1977

Virgin becomes the third label to sign Sex Pistols. A re-pressing of the scandalous 'God Save The Queen' is hit by delays after pressing plant workers refuse to produce the record; it

"EVER GET THE FEELING
YOU'VE BEEN CHEATED?"

JOHNNY ROTTEN, SEX PISTOLS VOCALIST

and subsequently banned by Boots, WHSmith and Woolworths. A Virgin Records store in Nottingham wins the right to display the contentious album after an indecency case is thrown out of court – the word "bollocks" is found to be an old English word meaning "small ball". Adverts for the record are also banned, which does not stop it sailing to number one.

## January 1978

Sex Pistols embark on a disastrous US tour. Sid Vicious' behaviour becomes increasingly unhinged, thanks in no small part to his chronic heroin addiction. During the final tour date in San Francisco, Johnny Rotten asks the crowd, "Ever get the feeling you've been cheated?" and leaves the stage after one song. The band splits.

## October 1978 – February 1979

Sid Vicious' girlfriend Nancy Spungen is found stabbed to death in New York's Chelsea Hotel. Vicious is arrested and subsequently released on bail. In December, he becomes involved in a physical altercation that lands him back in jail for 55 days. He detoxes while incarcerated, but overdoses upon his release on 1st February 1979. His body is found the next day. He is 21.

## June 1996

The original four Sex Pistols stage the first of many reunion concerts.

## January 2004

John Lydon appears on *I'm A Celebrity…Get*

eventually comes out at the end of the month. The song's lyrics ('God save the queen/She ain't no human being/And there's no future/ In England's dreaming') result in many shops refusing to stock the single, as well as a nationwide radio ban. The release is timed to coincide with Queen Elizabeth II's Silver Jubilee and sells over 150,000 copies. Amid claims that the charts have been rigged, 'God Save The Queen' is kept from the top by Rod Stewart's 'I Don't Want To Talk About It'.

## October 1977

The band's iconic debut album *Never Mind the Bollocks, Here's the Sex Pistols* is released

ABOVE: Johnny Rotten.

# TV FURY OVER ROCK CULT FILTH

CARPETED: Grundy

*Me Out Of Here!* and is famously attacked by ostriches. He also calls viewers "f****** c****" during a live broadcast.

## November 2006

Sex Pistols are inducted into the Rock & Roll Hall of Fame. They refuse to attend, calling the ceremony "a piss stain".

## October 2008

John Lydon becomes the new face of Country Life butter.

---

**A POP group shocked millions of viewers last night with the filthiest language heard on British television.**

The Sex Pistols, leaders of the new "punk rock" cult, hurled a string of four-letter obscenities at interviewer Bill Grundy on Thames TV's family teatime programme "Today".

The Thames switchboard was flooded with protests from angry viewers. Nearly 200 telephoned the Mirror. One man was so furious that he kicked in the screen of his £380 colour TV.

Grundy was immediately carpeted by his boss. Thames broadcast an official apology, and Grundy will make a personal apology in tonight's programme.

### Shocker

The show, screened live at peak children's viewing time, turned into a shocker when Grundy asked about £40,000 that the Sex Pistols are said to have received from their record company.

One member of the group said: "F——ing spent it, didn't we?"

Then when Grundy asked about people who preferred Beethoven, Mozart and Bach, another Sex Pistol remarked: "That's just their tough s——."

Grundy did not quite hear "tough s - - -" and insisted on its being

FOUL-MOUTHED: The Sex Pistols

**By STUART GREIG, MICHAEL McCARTHY and JOHN PEACOCK**

repeated until it was loud and clear.

Later he said: "Go on, you've got a long time. Say something outrageous."

A punk rocker replied: "You dirty bastard."

"Go on. Again." said Grundy.

"*You dirty f - - er*".

"What?"

"*What a f---ing rotter.*"

At that, Grundy said: "Well, that's it for to-night."

He told the viewers: "I'll be seeing you soon."

Then, turning to the group, he said: "I hope I'm not seeing you again."

*As the Thames switchboard became jammed, viewers rang the Mirror to voice their complaints.*

Lorry driver James Holmes, 47, heard the swearing being listened to by his eight-year-old son Lee and kicked in the screen of his TV.

"It blew up and I was knocked backwards," he said. "But I was so angry and disgusted with this filth that I took a swing with my boot.

"I can swear as well as anyone, but I don't want this sort of muck coming into my home at teatime.

"It's the stupidest thing I have ever done. I dread to think what my wife will do when she finds out about it."

Mr. Holmes, of Beechfield Walk, Waltham-Forest, Herts., added: "I am not a violent person, but I would like to have got hold of Grundy.

"He should be sacked for encouraging this sort of disgusting behaviour."

Stuart Simcox, of Palmers Green, London, said: "An apology is not good enough. Something more needs to be done."

Police Constable Alan Brown, of Hemel Hempstead, Herts., who was watching the programme with his wife and daughters, aged two and six, said: "Grundy was encouraging them to say the words."

### Sorry

Thames TV's current affairs controller, John Edwards, will hold an inquiry today.

He said: "Because the programme was live, we could not foresee the language which would be used. We apologise to all viewers."

*An IBA spokesman said: "It's inexcusable. We are sorry."*

Punk rock groups and their fans despise "establishment" pop stars and specialise in songs that preach destruction.

They dress as outrageously as possible with the aim of causing maximum shock.

## WHAT THEY SAID

THIS is some of the language that turned the air blue

**GRUNDY:** I am told that that group have received £40,000 from a record company. Doesn't that seem to be slightly opposed to an anti-materialistic way of life.

**SEX PISTOL:** The more the merrier . . .

**GRUNDY:** Tell me more then.

**PISTOL:** F—ing spent it didn't we?

**GRUNDY:** What about you girls behind . . .

**GIRL:** I've always wanted to meet you.

**GRUNDY:** Did you really. We'll meet afterwards shall we.

**PISTOL:** You dirty old man. You dirty old man.

**GRUNDY:** Go on, you've got a long time. Say something outrageous.

**PISTOL:** You dirty bastard.

**GRUNDY:** Go on. Again.

**PISTOL:** You dirty f—er.

**GRUNDY:** What?

**PISTOL:** What a f—ing rotter.

# MILLI VANILLI

Fab Morvan and Rob Pilatus – a.k.a. German pop duo Milli Vanilli – were a huge success story in 1988. Their debut single 'Girl You Know It's True' was an international smash, turning the two men into stars and resulting in a 1990 Grammy for Best New Artist. But a technical hitch would soon ruin their career.

Milli Vanilli's moment in the spotlight came to an abrupt halt during a mimed concert. Their vocal track became stuck, but an oblivious Fab and Rob carried on performing. When they realized their faux pas they fled the stage in disgrace.

The lip-synching debacle marked the beginning of the end for the group, as journalists began to question why Fab and Rob were not listed as vocalists on their album sleeve. German composer Frank Farian's role in Milli Vanilli also came into question, and he finally crumbled under pressure and admitted he was the voice of the group. Fab and Rob had been selected to "front" the project based purely on their looks and dancing abilities. The controversy resulted in Milli Vanilli's Grammy being revoked, while fans demanded refunds after claiming they had been defrauded.

The next record was credited to "The Real Milli Vanilli" and featured the actual vocalists on the front cover, while Fab and Rob unsuccessfully

**FANS who were duped by pop fakes Milli Vanilli are about to come in for a massive money refund.**

German-born duo Rob Pilatus and Fabrice Morvan had a soaring pop career until they were involved in a scandal which revealed they didn't sing on their songs and mimed to their best-selling videos.

The cheating pair were last year stripped of a prestigious Grammy music award for Best New Artist by pop bosses after they confessed to their deceit.

Now a court in Chicago has ruled that Milli Vanilli's American record company is liable to repay up to £15 million to angry fans who have launched a string of lawsuits over the affair.

Ten million fans worldwide shelled out more than £70 million buying Milli Vanilli's smash hit album *Girl You Know It's True*.

Thanks to the court ruling American fans are now set to receive refunds of:

● £2 for each video or CD bought;

● £1.30 for each cassette and;

● 60 pence for each album or single.

But British fans face a wait while lawyers and record company chiefs decide if fans can claim a refund in this country.

A spokesman for Milli Vanilli's British record company stayed silent last night. He said: "We can make no comment about the matter at the moment."

As part of the settlement the duo's record company has also been ordered to pay £160,000 to various charities.

The disgraced pair, who earned £2 million each from their hits, now call themselves Rob and Fab and are planning to make a movie based on the miming scandal.

# FAKES MILLI VANILLI WILL REFUND ANGRY FANS' CASH

# Mime doesn't pay

tried to re-launch using their own names and voices. The two men went through an acrimonious split but appeared to have settled their differences by 1997, when they re-grouped with Farian and plotted a comeback.

Sadly, the intervening years had not been kind to Rob, who had many run-ins with the law and a well-publicized battle with drugs. Just as Milli Vanilli prepared to return in 1998, he suffered an accidental overdose in a German hotel room. His death at just 33 put a permanent end to the Milli Vanilli reunion.

# MICHAEL HUTCHENCE AND PAULA YATES

Legions of music fans went into mourning in April 1997 when it was announced that heartthrob Australian rocker Michael Hutchence had passed away. The INXS frontman, famed for celebrity conquests such as Kylie Minogue, Helena Christensen and Paula Yates, was discovered in a Sydney hotel room having apparently committed suicide by

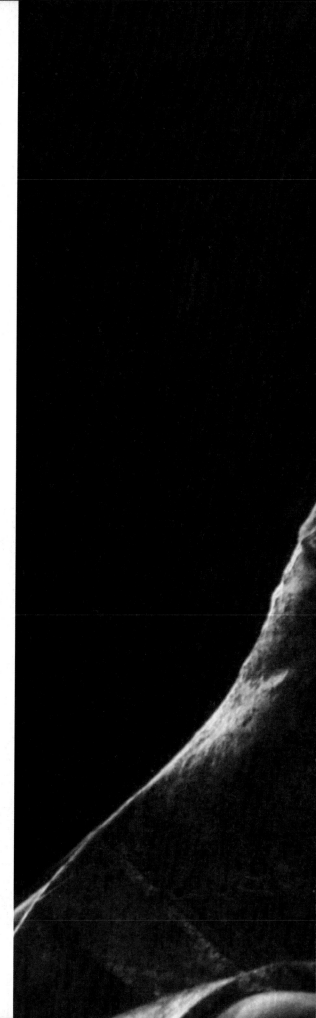

"IT'S JUST AS DIFFICULT TO
LIVE IN A SELF-MADE HELL
OF PRIVACY AS IT IS TO LIVE
IN A SELF-MADE HELL OF
PUBLICITY."

**MICHAEL HUTCHENCE**

hanging, though numerous sources close to Hutchence disputed this. The lack of a suicide note and the fact he was nude at the time of death led to speculation that he may have died from auto-erotic asphyxiation, a potentially fatal practice in which participants cut off the oxygen supply to the brain in order to gain sexual arousal.

Another factor that made his "suicide" unlikely was the fact that Paula Yates had given birth to his only child, Heavenly Hiraani Tiger Lily, the year before. Hutchence had been dating TV presenter Yates ever since she interviewed him on Channel 4's *Big Breakfast* in the mid-1990s, and their notoriously flirty exchange led to a passionate and well-publicized affair that marked them out as popular tabloid fodder. Yates – who was in the process of divorcing Boomtown Rats singer Sir Bob Geldof – soon fell pregnant, but Hutchence died less than a year after his daughter was born.

Yates fell into a deep depression after Hutchence's sudden and unexplained passing. She relapsed into drug abuse after a long period of sobriety and accidentally overdosed on heroin in 2000. Geldof was forced to fight for the right to adopt Tiger Lily so that she could stay with her three half-sisters, and was allowed to do so in spite of opposition from Hutchence's family. Her surname has since been changed to Hutchence-Geldof.

The Mirror

Friday November 28 1997

YOUR BIG VALUE PAPER FOR ONLY 30p

# GRIEF INXS

## SAD GOODBYE OF MICHAEL'S GIRLS

SEE PAGES 2, 3, 24 & 25

*Almost too much to bear...Paula Yates cradles daughter Tiger Lily at Michael Hutchence's funeral yesterday*

# GARY GLITTER

Gary Glitter's outlandish image and patented glam-rock sound made him a massive pop star in the 1970s. He sold over 18 million records, becoming the first artist to place his first 11 singles in the top 10, and even continued to score hits in the early 1990s with re-issues of his previous smashes. But despite his popularity he suffered a dramatic fall from grace in 1997 when 4,000 child pornography images were found on his personal computer.

# DEPRAVED

# NOWHERE TO RUN

## Desperate Glitter is shut out of Hong Kong

◄ LEERING Glitter on his way to Hong Kong yesterday

By KRISSY STORRAR

POP pervert Gary Glitter was running out of places to run last night in his desperate bid to avoid British justice.

Glitter, 64, was barred from entering Hong Kong after blagging his way on to a flight from Thailand. He wants to avoid being sent back to the UK, where he would immediately be put on the sex offenders' register.

He crowed: "I've been in jail three years. Now I want to do some shopping in Hong Kong."

But his plans were foiled when Chinese immigration chiefs refused him entry - and threat-

ened to have him sent straight back to Bangkok. He was in detention at Hong Kong airport last night while they decide what to do with him.

Meanwhile Thai authorities have declared him a persona non grata - and threatened to force him on to a plane to Britain if he returns.

**FULL STORY: PAGE 9**

208

Glitter – real name Paul Gadd – became public enemy number one after being found guilty of the crime. There was a huge public outcry when he was sentenced to just four months in prison, and although he was placed on the sex offenders register he was free to leave the country after serving his sentence.

Gadd set off for Cambodia, only to find himself being ordered to leave for posing a risk to children. As a result, he moved to Vietnam in 2002 – but didn't stay out of trouble for long; in 2005, he was arrested and charged for molesting two under-aged girls. The following year saw his conviction for committing obscene acts with minors, a crime that resulted in a three-year prison sentence.

Gadd was released from jail in 2008 and embarked on a brief game of cat-and-mouse with authorities as he tried to avoid returning to Britain. After failing to gain entry to Thailand and Hong Kong, a humiliated Gadd returned home. He was told in September 2009 that he was not allowed to leave the UK for a minimum of six months.

## BOY GEORGE

Former Culture Club frontman Boy George – real name George O'Dowd – has been involved with a number of scandals since bursting onto the pop scene in 1982. The flamboyant singer first ruffled the nation's feathers with his "gender-bending" image and ambiguous sexuality, repeating the trick in the mid-1980s when his drug addiction began to surface.

Signs that George was spiralling out of control appeared during an anti-racism concert in London. Fans were shocked by his bizarre performance and emaciated frame, and the tabloids began to speculate that he was suffering either from AIDS or drug addiction. In an alleged bid to save him, George was "outed" as a heroin addict by his own brother, but this was not enough to prevent the terrible news that keyboard player and Culture Club collaborator Michael Rudetski had suffered

# I DIDN'T LEAVE A JUNKIE TO DIE, SAYS BOY GEORGE

a fatal overdose at George's home. The subsequent investigation resulted in George's unusual charge for past-possession of heroin and a hasty spell in rehab.

George eventually cleaned up his act and carved out a successful new career as a DJ and writer, but in 2005 his drug problems resurfaced. Police were called to his Manhattan apartment to investigate a burglary, but when they arrived they found a confused George,

no burglary, and a small amount of cocaine. This episode resulted in a fine, community service and more rehab, but by 2008 he was back in the headlines after being accused of handcuffing and beating male escort Audun Carlsen. George was found guilty of the offence and sentenced to 15 months in prison, but was released after four months upon the condition that he adhere to a strict curfew and wear an ankle monitor for 90 days.

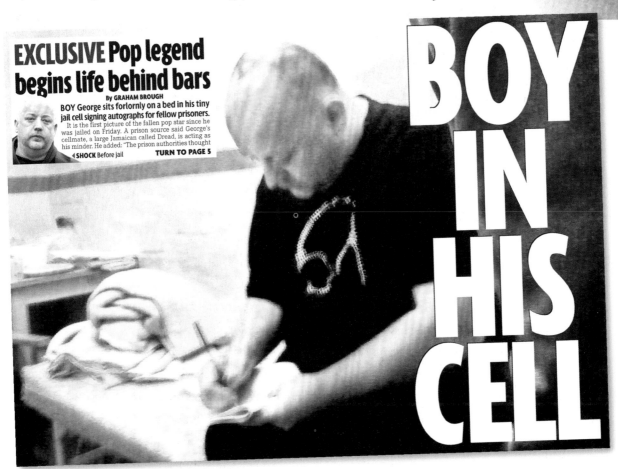

## EXCLUSIVE Pop legend begins life behind bars

By GRAHAM BROUGH

BOY George sits forlornly on a bed in his tiny jail cell signing autographs for fellow prisoners.

It is the first picture of the fallen pop star since he was jailed on Friday. A prison source said George's cellmate, a large Jamaican called Dread, is acting as his minder. He added: "The prison authorities thought

◄SHOCK Before jail

**TURN TO PAGE 5**

## BOY IN HIS CELL

# MICHAEL JACKSON

To fully grasp the unusual nature of Michael Jackson's childhood, one has to remember that he fronted the Jackson 5 – later known as the Jacksons – from the age of six onwards. At 11, he was named the youngest vocalist to top the US charts after 'I Want You Back' sailed to number one. Soon after, Motown records launched Jackson's solo career, which ran concurrently with his work in the Jacksons.

As he entered his teens it became apparent that Michael's bandmate brothers were trailing in his wake. He was the focal point of the group, and the number one target of their fans' affections. The mania that followed Jackson, however, caused him privately to retreat into his shell. His insecurities, instilled at a young age by his older brothers and father, Joseph, began to intensify. He started to wear make up both on and off stage in a bid to cover his teenage acne, and was disgusted by his brothers' treatment of the groupies that followed them everywhere.

Despite his unhappiness, Jackson's career continued to flourish. His 1979 album *Off The Wall* sold 20 million copies, while its follow up, *Thriller*, sold five times that amount. Jackson's position as the world's biggest star was cemented in 1983 when he unveiled the 'moonwalk' during a flawless performance of 'Billie Jean' at Motown's 25th anniversary concert. This spectacular dance move became Jackson's trademark and is still emulated today.

It was around this time that Michael Jackson's appearance began to change. He

first underwent rhinoplasty in 1979 after breaking his nose during a dance routine, but the operation was botched and left him with breathing difficulties. A second, allegedly final attempt was said to have fixed the problem, but at one point Jackson also had a cleft inserted into his chin for cosmetic purposes (something he later discussed in his 1988 autobiography, *Moon Walk*.) An accident on the set of a Pepsi commercial in 1984 left Jackson with second-degree burns to the scalp, and subsequently his Afro hair never looked the same again. By the time the *Bad* album was released in 1987, Jackson was unrecognizable from the fresh-faced African-American teenager who graced the cover of *Off The Wall*. His skin was noticeably lighter – something he attributed to the condition vitiligo, as well as the medicines used to treat it – and his features had assumed an androgynous look. Although Jackson tried to brush off the scandalous whisperings about plastic surgery, skin bleaching and eating disorders, it was too late – the British press had dubbed him "Wacko Jacko" and the name stuck.

Between the release of *Thriller* and *Bad*, Jackson began to enjoy playing the role of bizarre pop star, and regularly contributed to his own mythology. He bought a pet chimp named Bubbles, taking the creature everywhere and failing to deny rumours that they shared a secret language. He posed inside a hyperbaric oxygen chamber and falsely claimed to sleep in it every night in a bid to reach 150 years of age. Stories like this seemed fun to Jackson, and undoubtedly increased his record sales – but soon he was unable to stop the rumour mill, and he grew to detest the Wacko Jacko moniker. His cause was not helped by a decision in 1988 to purchase a multi-million dollar ranch, re-

naming it Neverland and placing both a fully functioning zoo and amusement park within its grounds.

Jackson clearly adored Neverland. He claimed to be at his happiest when the children who gathered outside his gates were let inside and allowed to play in the kingdom he had created. He staged charity events for needy children and organized sleepovers at his house. Although for some his behaviour was starting to become a cause for concern, Jackson maintained that his actions were innocent, claiming he simply preferred the company of children to adults. Many speculated that he was recreating the childhood he had never experienced, but this apparently blissful situation was not to last.

In 1992, Jackson struck up a year-long friendship with 12-year-old Jordie Chandler. He lavished gifts upon the boy and his mother, with the pair effectively living at Neverland for a time and becoming a surrogate family for Jackson. Jordie's dentist father Evan Chandler, who was separated from the boy's mother, began to voice his suspicions about the arrangement. He was unhappy that Jordie and Jackson had taken to wearing matching outfits, and extremely concerned to learn that Jordie had apparently slept alongside Jackson in bed.

It has been alleged that Chandler was removing a tooth from his son when he asked if there was anything improper about Jackson's behaviour. A medicated and woozy Jordie apparently confirmed his father's suspicions, causing Chandler to report Jackson. The scandal went global almost immediately and Neverland was searched with a fine-toothed comb, including Jackson himself enduring a humiliating strip search as a result of Jordie's description of the singer's genitalia. Neither

**The Jackson 5.**

investigation provided any evidence to support Jordie's claims. Jackson repeatedly proclaimed his innocence, and no charges were brought. Chandler did not give up easily though, launching a civil suit that Jackson opted to settle out of court for a rumoured $20 million. This decision may have ended the controversy in Jackson's eyes, but the public wanted to know why an innocent man would pay the Chandler family to disappear. It could easily be argued that Jackson's career and mental health never fully recovered from the 1993 scandal.

In the aftermath of the Jordie Chandler controversy, Jackson surprised his family, friends and fans by getting married – twice. His first bride was Lisa Marie Presley, daughter of Elvis and Priscilla Presley. Their 1994 marriage ended after 19 months when she refused to bear his child over fears he was too childlike himself. Jackson allegedly issued an ultimatum that he would find a surrogate if Presley wouldn't meet his demands. She called his bluff and Jackson sought a surrogate. Surprisingly, they divorced on amicable terms and remained friends.

Jackson arranged for his next wife, nurse Debbie Rowe, to give him two children via artificial insemination. Once Prince Michael and Paris were born – in 1997 and 1998 respectively – Rowe and Jackson divorced, with Rowe handing full custody to her ex-husband. Although this arrangement seemed odd, Jackson appeared to be very happy, and in 2002 a third baby arrived. In typically bizarre style, Jackson never revealed the mother of Prince Michael II, choosing instead to announce his arrival by dangling him over a fourth-floor balcony in Berlin. Once again, "Wacko Jacko" hit the headlines – video footage showed that the wriggling baby was perilously close to

slipping from his father's arms and into the crowd below. However, this scandal seemed positively minor in comparison to the outrage provoked by Jackson the following year.

In 2003, Jackson allowed British broadcast journalist Martin Bashir into his home. Bashir wanted to shadow the star and make a show that lifted the lid on the "real" Jackson. The programme *Living with Michael Jackson* included footage of his gargantuan spending sprees, as well as a startling interview in which a calm and unrepentant Jackson discussed the sleepovers he continued to have with children. At one point, a young cancer sufferer named

ABOVE: **Lisa Marie Presley and Michael Jackson.**

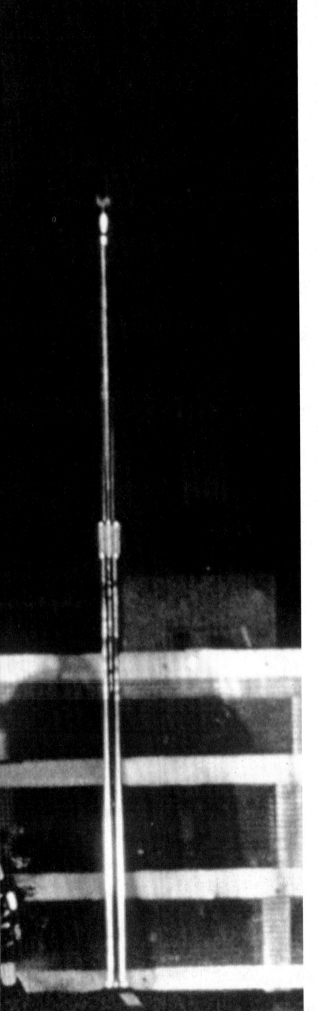

Gavin Arvizo sat on Jackson's lap in scenes that shocked viewers and dredged up memories of Jordie Chandler's allegations. When asked by Bashir if he couldn't see why his behaviour was worrying, Jackson replied: "It's very loving. What's wrong with sharing a love?"

After the show aired, a furious Jackson claimed that Bashir had deliberately edited the material to portray him in a negative light, and released his own footage that showed Bashir praising Jackson's parenting abilities. This wasn't enough to stem the growing public outcry though, and in November 2003 police descended on Neverland for a second time. Arvizo, it transpired, had accused Jackson of sexual abuse. The singer was eventually charged with seven counts of child molestation and two counts of administering an intoxicating agent. A tenth charge of conspiring to abduct a child was added later.

The People of the State of California v. Michael Joseph Jackson trial began in early 2005. Jackson, who appeared confident at the outset, began to wither away in front of the cameras. He relied heavily upon prescription painkillers throughout and seemed unable to concentrate as 135 witnesses and more than 1,000 pieces of evidence passed through the court. Several journalists noted that he appeared to be undergoing a complete mental and physical breakdown in front of the world's media.

Although things were looking extremely grim for Jackson, he was acquitted of all charges in June 2005. It wasn't all good news, however – his finances were in ruins, he hadn't had a hit record for years and he was on the verge of losing Neverland. On top of this, Jackson now appeared totally estranged from his family. They later claimed that a sinister

# JACKO DEAD

## King of Pop killed by heart attack at 50

group of enablers had moved in on Jackson, keeping him intoxicated and cut off from trustworthy acquaintances in order to fully exploit his estate.

Jackson's financial problems grew more desperate and complicated, and in late 2008 he announced plans to stage an auction of the contents of Neverland, including millions of dollars worth of antiques and original Michael Jackson paraphernalia. The items went on public display, but Jackson unexpectedly decided to halt the sale at the eleventh hour by suing the auction house, Juliens. They were baffled by this about-turn, but he was successful in his bid to keep the goods. Behaviour like this had long ceased to be shocking for Jackson, but the announcement of a comeback tour shortly afterwards definitely caused a sensation. Jackson, who hadn't performed since 1997's *HIStory* tour, had signed up with promoters AEG for a 10-night residency at London's O2 arena.

The *This Is It* dates were billed by Jackson himself as his "final curtain call", and sold out immediately. The residency was extended to 50 nights, a staggering run that was scheduled to continue well into 2010. Even his die-hard fans were wary of this development – Jackson still appeared frail and unpredictable, and rumours began to spread that he was failing to attend rehearsals. The postponement of the first few dates exacerbated fears that Jackson simply wasn't up to the job. British tabloids speculated wildly on the nature of the shows, and even

alleged that Jackson's contract only required him to be on stage for a minimum of 13 minutes per night. But such talk instantly evaporated when news broke that Jackson had been rushed to hospital in Los Angeles.

On 25th June 2009, mere weeks from the commencement of the *This Is It* residency, Jackson collapsed at his rental property in LA. A personal physician named Dr Conrad Murray had alerted emergency services after failing to resuscitate Jackson, and paramedics immediately transported the unconscious singer to the Ronald Reagan UCLA Medical Center. Around an hour later – just two hours after Jackson's doctor had called 911 – his death from cardiac arrest was confirmed.

As in life, Jackson was causing a scandal. It seemed unthinkable that the world's most famous entertainer could pass away at such a young age, just one day after attending an energetic rehearsal. Fans demanded to know how he had passed the medical tests required for his final concerts to go ahead. Police discovered propofol – a dangerous intravenous anaesthetic normally used in controlled medical environments only, and also known as Diprivan – in his home, and his death from "acute propofol intoxication" was eventually ruled as homicide by the Los Angeles coroner. A number of other drugs were also found in his system, including the stimulant Ephedrine, sedatives Midazolam and Diazepam and the painkiller Lidocaine. The investigation into his death is ongoing.

Jackson was buried on 3rd September 2009. He would have been 51 on 29th August.

# THIS IS IT

**EXCLUSIVE**

From TOM BRYANT in Los Angeles

MICHAEL Jackson will today be buried in a private funeral at a cemetery for the stars.

His three children are likely to attend the service at sprawling Forest Lawn in Los Angeles. But ex-wife Debbie Rowe snubbed an invite.

Later, Jacko's army of fans will say farewell to their idol at his memorial gig. Britain's Got Talent sensation Shaheen Jafargholi, 12, will sing the

**TURN TO PAGE 5**

▲ SINGING Shaheen

▶ **World bids huge farewell to Jacko today**

▶ **His kids at funeral but ex Debbie snubs it**

▶ **Britain's Got Talent Shaheen sings at tribute**

With special thanks to Michael Throne

Additional thanks to:
Adam Vaigncourt-Strallen
The Bell Lomax Moreton Agency